THE ELEPHANT LADY
of Thailand

A TRUE STORY

DENNIS W. SHEPHERD

The Elephant Lady of Thailand

A True Story

Dennis W. Shepherd

The Elephant Lady of Thailand

ALL RIGHTS RESERVED
No part of this book may be reproduced or transmitted in any form or by any means, electronic or mechanical, including photocopying, recording, or by any information storage and retrieval system, without permission in writing from the author, except in the case of brief quotations embodied in reviews.
Author hereby retains all rights to the work not specifically granted to the Publisher such as movie and screenplay rights.
Dennis W. Shepherd ©2010

Dedication: This book is dedicated to a little boy named Gingmai who lives in heaven now, but whose spirit surrounds Lek Chailert. It is also dedicated to a little girl named Samantha who lives in my heart.

The Elephant Lady of Thailand

The elephant has always been revered as a national symbol in Thailand. 1869 Photo of elephant of the royal family.

Dennis W. Shepherd

Prologue

The little hill tribe girl, perhaps seven years of age, went down the mountain, a few hundred yards from her jungle village to play in the creek below. A little girl and little creek fish, more like minnows, that she tried to catch in her hands. It was a bright sunny day, unusually bright because the sun was able to penetrate the high jungle trees. The girl skipped a stone across the creek, letting out a laugh it hopped. Then, in an instant, there was darkness, the sun blotted out, the little girl covered up by shade.

Surprised, she slowly moved her eyes up, toward the sun, trying to see what had turned her day so dark. As her head turned, she heard a deep growl, the kind of sound her pet cats made only much deeper and much more powerful. Her eyes reached the face of the animal that stood between her and the sun. It was the face of a giant Asian tiger.

The little girl froze, her face just inches away from the face of the tiger. The great animal moved its head sharply, perhaps trying to elicit a response from its prey. The little girl remained frozen with fright. With a huge paw, the tiger struck the air in front of its victim's face. Still the girl did not move. He then slowly turned away and walked back into the jungle.

The Tiny Moonlight Girl

This is the story of a beautiful woman who grew up loving elephants so much that she dedicated her life to saving them from pain and cruelty. Born in a village almost buried by the mountain jungle of northern Thailand, she fought many battles. She struggled against those who would look down their noses on a hill tribe girl. She walked several miles each way on mountain paths just to get to the local grade school. But it was her fight to save elephants that really defined her. Most of this book is devoted to that battle, or more accurately, to that *war*.

This is Sangduen's story. In the English language "Sangduen" is pronounced SANG (rhymes with rang) + DOO+WHEN. Some years after she was born, Sangduen's mother told her the story of her name. The name has a special meaning in the Thai language. Sangduen means moonlight. Her mother told her that on the night she was born there was a full moon. Under normal conditions in her jungle home, that is, when the moon was not full and shining brightly, a fire had to be lit to see anything. Fuel for the fire, besides wood, came from the natural resins or sap from jungle trees. But on the night Sangduen was born, the moon was so bright that no fire was necessary. Thus, she became the girl known as "Moonlight" or Sangduen.

Sangduen is the given name for the elephant lady. As is common in Thailand, she also earned a nickname. Miss Moonlight became "Lek," a common Thai name. Even though it is spelled L-e-k, it is pronounced somewhere between the English word lake and the sound of the first syllable of lecture. Lek means small. It is similar in meaning with another Thai word, *nidnoy*. Lek was nicknamed "little one" for good reason. When she was born beneath that bright full moon, she weighed less than four pounds.

Lek's Mountain Tribe

Lek comes from one of the many hill tribes of northern Thailand. These tribes are like the tribes of Native American Indians in the United States. The culture and beliefs of hill tribe people are very different from the general population of Thailand. Religious beliefs are different. An estimated ninety percent of the Thai population practices Buddhism. Members of the various hill tribes believe in spirits and deities, mixed with the Buddhist teachings they learn in temple grade schools. They also believe in a very broad concept of the soul. They believe that the soul is not something found just in people, but in animals, in jungle plants, in rice, in the wind and rivers. Anything that brings them food and anything that touches their lives must possess a soul.

To an outsider, the northern Thai hill tribes have exotic, mysterious, even magical sounding names. One tribe is called the Thins. Another is called the Karen tribe. Lek knew many Karen people growing up, because there were many Karen villages near her own village. When she became an elephant lady it was Karen men who rode atop the elephants she cared for. Other hill tribes include the Lisu, the Hmong, the Yao, and the Lawa.

Lek's ancestors come from a tribe that came originally from Laos called the Khamu tribe. All of the tribes have their own unique customs. But most of the hill tribes have two things in common. First, they show the greatest respect for their oldest villagers, the so-called village elders. Old age means wisdom not feebleness. Second, and this too is somewhat exotic, mysterious, and magical to an outsider, *they believe in the spirit world*. Lek has practiced respect for her elders throughout her life, and one of her grandfathers has been her personal guiding light. As for spirits, jungle spirits have always been a part of her life!

Out of Laos

Northern Thailand is located between two other Asian countries. To the west lies Myanmar, once more popularly known by the name, Burma. It is still called that today by many. To the east is Laos, a country whose western border follows most of Thailand's eastern border. It was from northern Laos that Lek's paternal grandfather came to Thailand. Noom, as he was called, struck out on a great river adventure in a small boat. He was just sixteen years old and accompanied by his two younger brothers, ages twelve and fourteen. The three of them navigated the mighty Mekong River, a river regarded as the lifeblood of Asia. Like the Mississippi in the United States, or the Nile in Egypt, the Mekong is one of Asia's most important rivers, supplying water, fish, and irrigation to millions. Stretching from deep inside of China, from the mountains of Tibet to the southernmost reaches of Vietnam, it empties into the South China Sea.

For Noom, it was a natural waterway from northern Laos to northern Thailand. He left the Khamu tribe of Laos looking for a better place to live. Tragedy struck when the river claimed the life of the older of Noom's two brothers. The fourteen-year-old disappeared into the Mekong, never to be seen again. Still, Noom found his way into Thailand where the story of Lek, the future Elephant Lady of Thailand, would begin.

After a few years spent just trying to survive in the new land, Noom settled down in a mountainous region of the north, marrying a young Thai lady named Fong. Their small, very simple mountain house was the first of a handful of family houses that would grow into a village. As his family grew, so grew the tiny village, one hidden from the rest of the world by thick jungle. No roads led to the village. Trees and vines were everywhere. The sky was largely blotted out by dense jungle vegetation. Nighttime was a particularly perilous time. The few families that settled in Noom's village kept their children close to them at night, afraid that a wandering child might be dragged away by a tiger. The village was named Baan Lao, which, roughly translated, means home to those from Laos. It was. It was Noom's home.

Lek's uncle, Tui, brother of her mother, arranged the meeting between Lek's mother and father. In fact, he arranged the marriage in the traditional hill tribe way. Lek's father, named Sa-Nguan, never met her mother, Phong Sri, before marrying. Noom's brother decided the marriage would be good for the family and good for the village: it was that simple. From this hill tribe custom, came a marriage that produced two sons and five daughters. Sa-Nguan's firstborn was Lek's brother, Boonta (1959), followed by Lek (1961). She was followed by four younger sisters, Pha Nee (1963), Sakorn (1967), Phetrin (1970), and Wasana (1975), and one younger brother, Preecha (1965).

The Shaman of Baan Lao

Shamans are found in all parts of the world, not just in Asia. They have many roles, even regarded by some as wizards or mystics. They often serve as the village medicine men or healers just as Lek's grandfather did. Through years of experience and training, a shaman learns to understand the natural world around him. He, and in certain cultures, *she,* knows how to use local plants and herbs as medicine. Noom made regular trips into the jungle to gather medicinal herbs. Like many shamans, he studied under his shaman father.

Mixing herbal cures for the sick is only one part of being a shaman. A shaman also tries to heal the emotional hurt a family feels when a death occurs. Through special ceremonies and great mental energy, the shaman tries to reconcile the end of physical life, and the continuation of the soul, with the spirit world. This helps the grieving family come to closure after the death of their loved one. There are other shaman duties. From bringing rain to a drought-stricken land, to resolving boundary disputes, the shaman is the most respected person in a hill tribe village.

Noom performed his duties in all of these areas. He was the village doctor and veterinarian, the village judge, and the village holy man. No one could mistake this because he had the body of a shaman. From his neck to his feet, tattoos of holy words and holy symbols adorned his body. He dealt with the souls and spirits of the plants, animals, humans, rocks, mountains, sun, moon, stars, rivers, streams—and on and on—all of the things alive and not that formed the world around him. He spent his life trying to understand these souls and spirits. To him, they were everywhere. With great mental concentration, Noom could enter into trance-like states. Through higher states of consciousness, Noom sought to come face-to-face, or *face-to-spirit* with that other world. Over the years, no one in the region earned more respect than Lek's grandfather.

The Other Grandfather and History

Noom was Lek's grandfather on her father's side of the family. She never knew her grandfather on her mother's side, not even through photographs. He came to a very sad end. He lived during the time of the great world war known as World War II. This war exploded in 1939 and grew until the Allied Forces, led by Great Britain, France, and the United States, fought against the armies of Germany, Japan, Italy, and those forces that formed the Axis Powers.

This war touched the lives of many Thai. As part of their war plan, the Japanese Forces invaded the mainland of Asia, using the men of the countries they occupied as slave labor to build bridges and clear jungle paths. The Imperial Japanese Army came to the grandfather's village. All able-bodied males were taken. There was no warning. There were no exceptions. If a male, young or old, could hammer, dig, or carry a heavy load, he was taken. It did not matter who he was or what he did in the village. It did not matter how many children he left behind, or that his wife or mother was sick. Gone! More than that, tens of thousands of these kidnapped fathers and sons never made it back alive. Lek's other grandfather, her mother's father, was one of these men.

There is a well-known tourist site made famous for a railway bridge built during the war connecting Thailand with Burma. It is a bridge spanning the Kwai River, which flows out of the great Mekong. The movie, *The Bridge on the River Kwai*, describes the brutal conditions of the slave laborers used to build the bridge, although the film only describes the plight of Allied prisoners of war. There were other, so-called "death railway" labor camps, populated by thousands of Thai men snatched from their families by the Japanese army.

Over 200,000 Asian laborers were kidnapped or tricked into the Imperial Army's slave labor camps, sometimes joining Allied prisoners of war, all working to build the Thailand-Burma Railway. Approximately 100,000 of the Asian slave laborers died from disease, torture, and physical abuse. Accurate records of these men, women, and children do not exist. No record exists for precisely what happened to Lek's maternal grandfather. To hide the atrocities, the Japanese Army buried the dead in mass graves, many of which may never be found.

Lek's other grandfather, who Lek remembers as "Mr. Kham," was kidnapped from his village and taken to a slave labor camp. He died building a bridge in the northern Thai province of Mae Hongson. News of his death eventually reached Lek's grandmother, Thiang. Soon after hearing it, she too died. The medical cause of her death was disease. But to her family, she died of a broken heart. The war was cruel to Lek's mother, making her an orphan.

Noom, on the other hand, survived the war. But even he did not escape the hand of the invading Japanese. He too was ordered to serve the Imperial Japanese Army. But, as young as he was, just in his thirties when the war began, he was able to avoid the death camps because of his special skills as a medicine man.

The Golden Elephant

There is no accurate marker that indicates when Lek felt her calling to save elephants from pain. Like so many life-changing events and decisions in life, it just happened. But one event that moved her toward this calling was the first time an elephant entered her world.

Lek spent most of her childhood learning from her grandfather, Noom. Her mother was always there, but it was from Noom that she wanted to learn. He was such a special, unique individual because he was the shaman. Her father, Sa-Nguan, was also there during her childhood, but he often worked outside of the village. He was busy raising her older brother,

The Elephant Lady of Thailand

Boonta, since he, as the oldest male, would be expected to help the family the most. Lek and her grandfather became inseparable. Yet, it was at a time when the two were separated, that an elephant walked into her life.

One day, when Lek was just five or six, Noom was called away to another village. A young boy was seriously ill. At the time the shaman of Baan Lao was already well known beyond his own village, even outside his own Khamu hill tribe. The head of a Karen hill tribe village asked Noom to help cure his son. The son had gotten so ill, most thought he would soon die. Noom traveled back and forth between Baan Lao and the Karen village. He would spend a few days treating the sick boy, and then return. Soon, he was back with the sick son. This went on for several weeks.

During one of his absences, a very strange and wonderful thing happened. Lek saw a giant of an elephant enter Baan Lao. Atop the huge creature sat a mahout of the Karen tribe. A mahout is the driver, keeper, and trainer of an elephant. In northern Thailand, mahouts are usually members of one of the hill tribes. Lek watched as the Karen mahout rode the elephant into Baan Lao, stopping at Noom's house. He announced to the family that, from that day on, the elephant belonged to them. Lek was stunned. She was excited beyond belief, but her excitement would not last long.

Lek asked the mahout how to care for the elephant. She was going to take charge, even at such a tender age. She learned that this elephant was a female of about sixty years of age. She was most likely in her final years. Asian elephants usually don't live past their sixties. Lek wanted to know everything about the care and feeding of elephants, but most of all she wanted to know how to take care of THIS elephant, HER elephant, and the beautiful animal that the jungle spirits seemed to magically send to her. She wouldn't stop asking questions until she knew everything there was to know about the new giant in her life.

The mahout was very patient and kind to the little Khamu moonlight girl. He answered all of her questions. He told Lek how the elephant behaved so Lek wouldn't be surprised by a sudden movement. He taught how to be gentle so nothing she did would cause the great animal to run. She quickly learned that this particular elephant had the friendliest nature imaginable. The elephant immediately took to Lek and the other village children. Soon she was carrying children on her back and allowing them to play with her while they screamed and shouted with laughter and joy. It was as if some unseen force commanded her, telling her to be especially gentle, safe, and patient with the little ones.

Lek had never felt anything like the love she felt for this magnificent creature. She loved her from the start. She and the other children stopped what they were doing, stopped thinking about anything else, after the elephant walked into their lives. They named her Chang Thongkam, or Golden Elephant. It was as if a great golden treasure came walking down the road one day, enriching all of their lives. Unfortunately, the good feeling would only last a few days.

The children rode her all day without tiring. This was so new to them. Their popular game of swinging on the jungle vines from tree to tree was quickly forgotten. Now they climbed up and rode on the golden elephant. Sometimes they crawled up from her front, up her trunk. Sometimes they pulled their way up using her tail. And for all of their jumping and climbing and pulling and shouting, Chang Thongkam never showed them anything but a loving back and steady body to climb, being the gentlest of giants.

Chang Thongkam changed everything in Baan Lao for the small children like Lek. She made them forget about things they did not have. Things like plentiful food. Things like electricity. Having a gigantic, lovable elephant made them think only of how lucky they were to have her. She even turned work into a happy thing. Like so many other Thai children living beyond the big cities, the children of Baan Lao had to help their families earn money and grow food. In the case of the village children, including Lek, this meant working in the rice fields.

Very early in the morning, families headed off to work in the water-filled rice paddies. Depending on the season, they would plant or weed or harvest. In the 1960s and 1970s, water buffaloes were used to pull the old-fashioned plows. They have since been replaced with motor-driven plows. For Lek and her little friends it was hard work, almost always under a burning sun. Chang Thongkam made it an adventure—a fun adventure. The children would ride atop her to get to their chores in the rice fields, singing as they went. After hours in the hot sun, working in the wet and muddy fields, and after being completely worn out from their work, they sang more songs on their way home.

Not all of the games they played with her were good ones. The children could be very rough with her, tugging her ears and pulling her tail. Khamu parents made their children toys from jungle vines, bamboo, or other jungle objects. Some made toy guns. Lek's brother, Boonta, would pretend to shoot Chang Thongkam with his toy gun. He even taught her to play dead as soon as he shot her. He knew Chang Thongkam sometimes would lie down for the kids and let them play games as if she was their fort or castle. After a few lessons, she did what Boonta wanted, falling down as gently as such a large animal could, just as soon as he pointed his gun and yelled "bang." When Lek's mother found out what kind of game this was, she stopped it. Even pretending to shoot the "golden one" was an affront to the spirits.

Three days after Chang Thongkam arrived in Baan Lao, Noom returned. When he heard what happened, he ordered the mahout to return Chang Thongkam to the Karen village. Lek could not believe it. Her heart was broken. In just three days she had grown to love "her" elephant. But Noom would not change his mind. To him, this elephant was a payment for his services as a shaman and he did not want that. Small tokens of appreciation he could accept, but not something as important as an elephant. He tried to explain this to Lek. An elephant in a Karen village, he told her, was extremely important to the people. They used her to help clear the jungle and pull heavy loads that the men could not handle without great effort. But all Lek understood was that her heart was broken in two. She loved Chang Thongkam and she was losing her. It was that simple.

Noom told his family that the head of the Karen village tried to give him the elephant while Noom was there, tending to the young boy. Noom refused to accept it then, and he would refuse it now. He had to send it back. It was a matter of principle. Curing people as a shaman must be according to the law of the jungle. It must be without payment. That is what the spirits of the jungle expected.

But something happened to change all of this. The Karen mahout spoke to Noom. He said the leader of the Karen village had been watching Noom as he used his shaman medicine on the boy, that is, on his own son. As he watched his son slowly get better, the father visited the nearby jungle. There he made a pact with the jungle spirit. Karen people believe in spirits and jungle ghosts in the same way as the Khamu hill tribe. The Karen leader promised the jungle spirit that he would give the elephant to the family of the person who could save his son. It was a sacred vow. After hearing this, Noom relented. Chang Thongkam could stay. She must stay. Powers greater than even a shaman had so decreed!

An Elephant Legend and the Golden One Swallows Lek's Baby Brother Whole

The children of Baan Lao grew up hearing many stories about jungle animals. One of the most popular was about an elephant, a mighty creature that worked for the king. Sitting atop his powerful elephant, the king fought many battles. In fact, he never lost with this elephant leading him into the fight. But as time went by, the great beast grew too old to fight. As he aged, the king no longer treated the elephant with respect. He no longer protected the once powerful elephant that helped him win so many battles. The people of this kingdom also lost respect for him. No one would care for him. No one fed him. It got much worse. As he walked with the slow-moving, heavy walk of the aging giant that he was, the people would beat him and even spit on him.

One day an old beggar found him. He fed him and took him to the river where he scrubbed the grateful elephant clean and made him feel wanted again. After caring for the elephant that no one else loved, the beggar awoke to a magnificent surprise. A large pile of gold was waiting for him. According to Khamu legend, the pile of gold was once a pile of elephant droppings. The old man continued to take care of the elephant even after his newfound gold. One day he awoke to a treasure chest of fabulous jewels. It seemed the more he loved the elephant, the richer he

The Elephant Lady of Thailand

became. But instead of keeping his riches, he spent the rest of his life giving them away to the poor.

As the Khamu children played with Chang Thongkam, they thought about this legend and how their "treasure elephant" could make them rich. It was a silly thought that perhaps only poor Khamu children would ever think. But children can do very silly things and one day several of the children began looking into the mouth of Chang Thongkam. They peered in to see if just maybe some of the gold might be down there. One of the youngest, Lek's little brother, Preecha, then not quite three, was one of the curious lookers. Older children helped him up and into the elephant's huge mouth. The other children told him to look down Chang Thongkam's throat to see if gold was hidden in her stomach.

In Preecha went, happy to be the one chosen to look for something so wondrous as gold! Wider and wider the children opened the elephant's mouth. Half of Preecha's little body disappeared down the elephant's throat. The golden one was accommodating, holding her mouth wide open in one gigantic yawn. Soon more than half of Preecha went inside her throat—then more.

All of a sudden, the elephant gave a great shake. Her mouth began to move in spastic contractions. Little Preecha was nearly gone, with Chang Thongkam unable to hold off the inevitable. Half trying to throw up and otherwise trying to relieve cramping jaw muscles, she had to close her mouth all the way!

At this very moment, Lek's mother saw what was happening. She was in the kitchen looking at her son falling down the elephant's throat. She saw the children about to make the elephant's mouth contract and vomit. The muscles in the elephant's jaws were about to pull Preecha in, sucking him into the belly of Chang Thongkam. Phong Sri ran up to Chang Thongkam, reached far down her throat, and grabbed Preecha. She pulled for dear life and Preecha was saved. That was the end of the search for gold!

The golden elephant meant much more to Lek than rides and fun games. Through her, Lek learned how to love one of the jungle's most amazing creations. As old as she was, as large as she was, Chang Thongkam poured out her own love to Lek completely and instantly. Lek knew it was only right to return the love in the same way. This majestic and tender animal forever touched Lek in a way that is almost impossible to describe in words or explain with mere human explanations. Later, when Lek was grown, when she saw how elephants were tortured, the lessons of the golden elephant always returned. She knew she had a calling. She had no idea how to answer it, but in her heart she had to try.

The Little Doctor Breaks the Law of the Jungle

Lek was born beneath the bright light of a full moon. Perhaps the coincidence of her mother and the moon coming to full term on the same night has some special meaning in jungle lore. Born so small, she was called "little one." But how she earned another name, a name of high honor, is an entirely different story.

Grandfather Noom was more than a medicine man for the people of the village. Because he was the shaman, and a shaman must seek harmony with nature, Noom was also the village veterinarian. After all, to these hill tribe people, animals have souls just as humans do. Therefore, Noom used his special knowledge of jungle medicine to treat sick and injured animals. It was this part of his job that Lek loved the most. As soon as she could walk and talk, and follow her grandfather around Baan Lao, Lek learned how to nurse sick animals back to health. Some of her first lessons came when the golden elephant appeared. With Chang Thongkam, Noom showed Lek the things that must be done to keep the aging elephant alive and well, things like giving her jungle medicine to prevent worms, and feeding her the right food to improve her nutrition.

When Lek helped her grandfather treat an animal, Noom would call her his "little doctor." Every time she heard this, she swelled with pride. The village's most important man called her, the smallest child, doctor! This made her try harder and pay more attention to her work. Saving animals from pain and illness became her passion. Year after year, Lek learned more and more from Noom. But there was one lesson that nearly broke her heart.

The Elephant Lady of Thailand

When Noom asked Lek to go with him to collect herbs in the jungle, it was always an adventure. Noom made these trips each day, waking before the sun was up. Lek did not mind waking up so early. She was the little doctor and it was her job just as it was her grandfather's job. Even though this was Thailand, a country most people think of as hot most of the year round, this was not true in the mountains. For Lek, it was cool most of the time, and quite cold during Thailand's winter season. During her morning walks into the jungle with her grandfather, Lek could always expect chilly temperatures and a thick layer of mountain fog.

Deep into the jungle they would go, looking for medicinal plants before anyone else would even think of going there. When they had collected enough, they would return to Noom's medicine hut. In fact, Noom had built two huts. One hut was divided into four rooms, about nine feet by nine feet per room. This was his "patient" hut, where he received sick villagers for treatment. The second hut was well known by everyone in Baan Lao, if for nothing else, by its smell. From a great distance, villagers could smell the sometimes pungent but always-strong aromas of the various herbs stored there.

Occasionally, during one of their morning treks into the jungle, they would come upon an animal in a poacher's trap. Poachers tried to capture wild animals to sell in the city. Thailand was a poacher's dream, with so many exotic animals there for the taking. Many poachers did not care if their traps killed or tortured the animals. They only wanted something to sell. If the animal died, and thus was not worth anything, the poacher would simply toss the animal aside and set another trap.

Noom did not like to see animals in these traps. He never helped the poachers, but he often helped the trapped animals. Animals that did not seem to be seriously injured by the trap, Noom released back to the jungle. For the poor animals that were seriously injured by the trap, Noom could do nothing, not even with the powers of a shaman. But, the ones he could treat and help heal, he and the little doctor would take back to the village. It was helping Noom care for the injured animals taken back to Baan Lao that led to Lek's trouble with the law of the jungle.

One of her grandfather's most important rules was the hardest for Lek to follow: *Wild animals belong in the jungle where they came from.* It wasn't hard for her to understand this rule, just to obey it. It was long after her childhood days that Lek would understand the wisdom behind it. As a young girl treating the animals, growing close to them, and loving them, it was impossible for her to understand her grandfather's rule.

Two animals in particular became her favorites. More than favorites, they became part of her. One was a jungle squirrel and the other was a gibbon. Like any child with a pet, Lek did not want to give up her two animals. Nursing both back from injury made the bond between them all the stronger. When both were strong enough, Noom reminded her of the rule: *Wild animals belong in the jungle where they came from.*

Lek tried to do what her grandfather wanted, but it was so difficult. She spent so much time with them. They were hers now, not the jungle's. At least, that is what her child's mind told her. Noom had warned her. He told her not to handle them, not to pet them. But she could not resist. When she hugged them, they seemed so happy. Grandfather also warned her not to keep them in her room, but she did. It was when Noom found out that the gibbon and the squirrel slept in her bed that he gave her a final order. *Release them to the jungle where they came from!*

At first, Lek, as small and as young as she was, tried to bargain with her grandfather. She gave him reasons for keeping the animals longer. There were hunters who would kill them. There were poachers who would continue to try to trap them. But Noom would not bargain. The rule of the jungle was clear. It was not his rule. It was nature's rule. Lek had to listen. Hurt but obedient, she released her squirrel and gibbon, back to the jungle where they were found. This should have ended her days as a violator, but it did not.

The more animals Lek released, the more she missed them. As she followed her grandfather into the jungle on their early morning herb-collecting trips, she looked for the chance to call to them. When Noom was busy with his herbs, she let out a whistle. Soon, one of her friends appeared. One by one, many eventually answered her call. When her grandfather realized that she had not given them up completely, he told her something that eventually struck deep in her heart. He told her that if she really loved them she would completely let them go. As long as they stayed in contact with her they would be out of harmony with the jungle. To ensure that her break with them was complete, Noom told her she must change her route and never try to find her animal friends again.

It would take her several years to understand this. In the meantime, in trying to follow the rules—the rules of her grandfather and the rules of nature—Lek felt the sharp pain of losing her jungle friends. It was as if something was leaving her body. With each animal she released, she felt part of her own being go with it. Releasing animals back to the jungle meant part of her soul went with them, deep into the jungle, high up on the mountain.

Her eyes reached the face of the animal that stood between her and the sun. [This is the actual site of the little girl's meeting face-to-face with the tiger as it appears today.]

The second hut was well known by everyone in Baan Lao, if for nothing else, by its smell. From a great distance, villagers could smell the sometimes pungent but always-strong aromas of the various herbs collected there.

Growing Up Khamu

Mornings during Lek's childhood in Baan Lao meant a very special wake-up call. She did not wake to the sound of a manufactured alarm clock. Instead, her alarm was a high-pitched whooping, joined by another, then another, back and forth, increasing in volume, until the entire jungle seemed to be crying out for attention.

The first chorus came from a soprano, yelping in long stretches: EEYOOP—EEYOOP—EEEEYOOOOP—EEYOOP-EEYOOP! This melodic hoot echoed loudly, piercing the thick jungle, sounding like an exotic bird singing at the top of her lungs.

A tenor's answer followed almost instantly, when another songster hooted back just as loudly as the first. But this time the singing stung the air in short bursts, and sounded like someone playing music on a saw: WOOP WOOP WOOWOO—WOOP WOOP WOOWOO—WOOP WOOP WOOWOO. The call and answer would then multiply as other singers joined the chorus, until Lek and everyone in the village could hear the jungle reverberate with the back-and-forth love song.

In a way it was a love song, but lovebirds did not make it. Lek awoke most mornings of her childhood to these sounds, the sounds of gibbons calling to each other. First, the female would declare her motherhood and strength: EEEYOOP—EEYOOP—EEEEYOOOOP—EEYOOP—EEYOOP! Her mate would answer. Once begun, other gibbons joined in until the power of the group vocals became deafening. In this way, the gibbons showed their unity. The whooping morning song declared to all: "This is my territory. Enter at your own risk!" This indeed was their territory. Trespassers, especially gibbons not in their group, would face the anger, and if necessary, a terrible violence from the present owners.

The villagers of Baan Lao had no such sense of ownership for their land, for their village, or even for their personal property. Because they were hill tribe people, other Thai, especially the city people, looked down upon them. Lek suffered many embarrassing moments just because she was born of a certain blood.

Lek knew from a very early age that her people were different. One day Grandfather Noom took her to see a road being built through the jungle by government workers. He wanted her to see the powerful tractor that dug up the land. He showed her something new, and at the same time, warned her that new is not always a good thing. As the tractor dug up the jungle, she could see how sad her grandfather was to see so many jungle plants being destroyed.

As Lek and her grandfather stood watching the powerful tractor, the man in charge of the road crew yelled at Noom to move out of the way. He called him "stupid Khamu." He cursed at him using the most vulgar curse word. All Noom could do was move away. As the village leader, he was greatly insulted by the worker. Despite his high standing in Baan Lao, when he faced someone deemed better than a hill tribe person, Noom sank to the lowest level of human beings. Other villagers from Baan Lao watched as the outsider rudely told Noom to move. It hurt Lek to know that a man as good and as respectable as her own grandfather could be treated so badly by strangers.

Dennis W. Shepherd

Lek the Wild Fox

Some of Lek's earliest and fondest memories of Baan Lao were of the many animals that lived in the surrounding jungle. Being an animal lover and a budding animal doctor, it was heaven on earth. Besides the gibbons that greeted her each morning, there were monkeys everywhere she went. Near the treetops she could sometimes spy what looked like a slow-moving monkey, inching along the branches, looking for bird eggs or insects to eat. It wasn't really a monkey at all, but another primate called the slow loris, distinctively marked with the black-eyed face of a raccoon.

The jungle that was Lek's childhood home was filled with wildlife. It was only later, after she embarked on her life's passion—to save elephants—that she appreciated the freedom these animals had before the jungle began to disappear. Freedom came from space. Space then meant hundreds of acres of mountains, jungles, rivers, and streams to wander. Later, when Lek founded her nature preserve for elephants, she would worry over the fact that her thirty or so "saved" elephants only had forty-four acres of land.

Natural enemies in the jungle of her childhood meant the great cycle of life—other than human beings with rifles! Fighting for survival in the natural habitat was fair because that was nature's way. Running from high-powered rifles was a necessity brought on by a disruption of the natural cycle. The jungle surrounding Baan Lao when Lek was a child was filled with wild animals. Tigers roamed the area, but only came into contact with humans by accident. Bears and deer were plentiful as were porcupines and all varieties of hornbill birds. Brown hawk owls from China migrated to the vicinity of Baan Lao to lay their eggs. As Lek grew up, she watched as roads, buildings, and machines stripped away the lush forest, exposing the animals to greater and greater danger.

As the jungle disappeared, so did the animals. As more people from the city came, the fewer animals there were. Outsiders would come and hunt the animals at will. Poachers would trap them to sell them in the city. The land around Baan Lao, first settled by Noom, and then by others of the Khamu tribe, was open to anyone for the taking. The Khamu had very little say in the matter. They were, after all, just hill tribe people.

Lek could always feel the difference. Even the livestock that the villagers needed for their own food, outsiders could take. She witnessed times when government officials entered Baan Lao and simply pointed to someone's pig, meaning it was now theirs. She watched as construction crews finished their work, and their crew leader ordered the villagers to prepare a pig roast so they could celebrate the end of their work. It was all very shameful. But nothing was more shameful than the way Lek was treated as she fought to get her education.

Overcoming her parents' will was her first challenge. They did not believe that girls should go to school. Girls belonged at home, learning the many chores involved in caring for a husband, for children, and for the rest of a Khamu family. But Lek would not and could not accept this. She had a burning desire to go to school no matter how difficult that would prove to be. School meant doing something that very few Khamu could do. It meant showing other non-Khamu Thai that a hill tribe girl could succeed. It was this desire that convinced her parents to abandon their own plans and let Lek enter the non-hill tribe world.

Finding a school in the middle of the jungle was her next challenge. Like most of the children of the village, Lek first attended a school run by the local temple, named Wat Baan Lao. The temple was close, barely a half-mile from Lek's house, at the top of a hill. Here, monks of the temple taught children younger than seven the most basic things, like the Thai alphabet and simple lessons in mathematics. The children of Baan Lao attended the temple school more as a place to meet and play with other children than to learn. One day Lek overheard a visitor to the temple school. He was talking to the monk teachers and Lek heard him ask why the monks were wasting their time teaching Khamu children. He said it was like teaching a monkey to make jewelry. Lek saw his angry eyes looking at her and the other Khamu students with disgust.

When she was six, and still going to the temple school, Lek saw something amazing while out picking leaves in the jungle with her mother. A bird flew so high above them that it was nearly invisible. Its shiny silver body reflected the sun like a mirror. Her mother told her it was an iron bird, and tried to explain that what she saw was an airplane, filled with people on their way to a far off destination. Lek refused to believe anything made of iron could fly, but she promised her mother that one day she would find the iron bird and learn what made it float so effortlessly among the clouds. To Lek, there was only one way to solve this mystery. She had to go to school.

Upon turning seven, the law required attendance at a government-run school. The closest such school was nearly nine miles from the village. It was nine miles through jungle paths, and up and down a mountain. The walk was difficult. Walking barefoot made it all the more so. Khamu kids like Lek did not have shoes. Her mother did not worry about the animals she might meet along the way. Lek's parents and Grandfather Noom taught her that wild animals do not hurt humans who stay out of their territory. They did worry about the floods. It was not uncommon for a flash flood to sweep through the area after a monsoon rain. Very few villagers knew how to swim, and floods had killed some in the past. They also worried about one more thing: *humans*.

Three days each week, Lek set out on a long walk through the mountain paths to attend the government school. She walked with a few other village kids, all of them boys. No other girl from Baan Lao went. Little Lek, the moonlight girl, stood out as a very different student. When she arrived at the school, the battle was not won; it had only begun.

Children can be cruel. They are just children, but they sometimes take on the meanness of their families. It was not different at the school. Just as the government worker had insulted Baan Lao's shaman with mean words and demeaning orders, the children of the school picked on Lek without mercy. Because the hill tribe kids did not have shoes, the other children made fun of them. One day, a boy from the city came up to Lek. He looked down at her bare feet. He told her that he heard Khamu kids had extra tough skin. He then stepped on her bare foot with his shoe until she cried in pain.

During the years she spent attending the government school, Lek suffered many embarrassing moments. One day for instance, a boy tried to peek into her dress. He heard that Khamu children wore no underclothes. When Lek complained to the teacher, nothing was done. The boy was the teacher's son.

The walk to school meant that Lek would have to pass through thickets and brush when the narrow paths disappeared. It meant that the morning dew from the trees and bushes she passed would sometimes rub against her and wet her school blouse. One day she stopped outside of the school to sun herself, letting the sun dry her clothes. When they were dry, Lek started for her classroom when a boy surprised her, dousing her with water. He thought it was funny. Lek did not and began to fight him. One of the boy's friends joined in, trying to help him beat the little Khamu girl, but Lek proved too much for even two boys. She won the fight, or so it seemed. When her teacher heard what happened, she ordered Lek to be punished! With a bamboo whip, the teacher struck Lek several times, opening the skin on the last blow.

After so many battles, Lek earned a new nickname. She wasn't the moonlight girl, or the little one. She wasn't the little doctor. The children teased her by calling her the wild fox. They meant it as an insult. They wanted her to feel like a wild animal, not a child. When Lek could not take it any more, she told her mother what was happening to her in school.

She waited a very long time before revealing the taunts and teasing to her mother. The fights did not scare Lek. The insults from other children and sometimes the teacher: those did not bother her. It wasn't the fights or teasing that Lek feared most, it was the threat of not being able to stay in school. She wanted to go to school, no matter how difficult it became. Something deep inside of Lek yearned to learn more. As Noom's chosen apprentice, she loved learning about the world around her. Inside a small school classroom, with no air conditioning, and an old chalkboard, she could know what the other kids knew, the ones not born of hill tribe parents.

Another battle began on a day when Lek was feeling sick to her stomach. As she sat in her class, she put her head down she felt so bad. When she did some boys pounced on her, cutting her long hair off. Then they danced around singing, "a fox with no tail, a fox with no tail." Lek fought once again for her honor.

Once again the teacher punished her, beating her for fighting. Even during the teacher's beating, Lek refused to cry.

Chickens Don't Smoke Cigarettes

After nearly a year of facing daily teasing and insults, Lek could not hold it back any longer. She poured her heart out to her mother. She begged her to allow her to stay in school. But Lek confessed that it hurt her badly to be called a name like wild fox. Sometimes, she told her mother, they called her the dirty fox. When they drenched her dress by throwing water on her, they called her the fox that fell in the river. Despite this, she did not want to give up. School meant everything to Lek. The pain of growing up as a hill tribe girl was always there and sometimes became unbearable. She looked into her mother's eyes, searching for an answer, any answer that might give her the strength to continue.

Her mother understood. She was a very wise and loving parent. She had no intention of taking Lek out of school. But she had to show her daughter that, as difficult as it was, she could succeed. She offered her daughter a simple lesson about names.

"Chickens never smoke cigarettes," Lek's mother told her. At first Lek was surprised by her mother's strange words.

"Elephants never drink alcohol," she said. "Monkeys don't use opium." Her mother explained that one of the worst offenses in the land was to call someone you did not like, or someone you thought was evil, by an animal's name. This wasn't right, and it made little sense considering that nearly all of the animals near Baan Lao were useful in some way to the villagers. Lek's mother told her one more thing: "Always stand up and fight for your tribe. Being part of the Khamu people is something to be proud of, not something to be ashamed of." Lek was fighting for her people every time she fought against the kids who insulted her.

In the many years that passed, after growing up Khamu, and fighting so many battles, her mother's words would come back to Lek like golden nuggets of wisdom. Of all the things in her childhood that were precious and good, the animals stood out. They were the little doctor's injured patients. They were the wild animals that wandered near Lek and her grandfather as they walked through the fog in the early morning. The one thing that she could always enjoy was the beauty of these animals. To be called a wild one, and a fox at that, was something she could take as a mark of honor. The children who called her names did not understand that. They were ignorant. But with her mother's help, Lek knew what was right and that's all that mattered. To her mother, Lek was not an animal but a princess. To Lek, her mother was her guardian angel. And nothing, but nothing would ever change that.

The Spirit of the Jungle

The world is filled with beliefs. Science is belief in earthly knowledge and truths. Religion is belief in divine knowledge and truths. But in Lek's world, the world she knew growing up, what she and the other Khamu believed came from the world around them. Science had little to do with it. Outside forces had little to do with what the men, women, and children of Baan Lao believed. Buddhism had some influence, especially its belief in karma. The real world for the Khamu, the one that taught them right from wrong, the one that guided them in life, and the one that explained what happened in death, that world was all around them. It was the jungle. It was the wind, the plants, the fog, the trees, and the animals. It was the entire jungle universe of living and nonliving matter surrounding each hill tribe being. Love began with that world. Hope came from the jungle. Wealth was measured in how close you were to nature and how well you understood a special force called the spirit of the jungle.

During her walks in the jungle, Lek heard many stories from her grandfather. Sometimes they were simple lessons about the different plants they would find there. He told her how to survive if she ever got lost in the jungle. He warned her of the plants she could not eat. He showed her which mushrooms she could eat and which ones would make her deathly ill.

Cooking in the jungle was also a lesson taught by Grandfather Noom. He showed her how to wrap jungle vegetables inside of banana leaves and roast them. Other food could be cooked inside of a stalk of bamboo. She learned all of the ways of the Khamu. She could even coat vegetables in mud, and then roast them over a fire. Wild mushrooms and wild potatoes were everywhere in the jungle. Noom taught her that there was no reason to go hungry, even if you were lost and all alone. But it was Noom's stories about jungle spirits and ghosts that Lek loved the most. These became a source for her own love of nature.

Lek learned about the importance of the trees. They were more than just trees. They were life. They were the jungle's lifeblood and life force. They were art. They represented the beauty of nature. Noom spent many lessons teaching Lek about them.

He told her to bring home five different tree leaves from each walk in the jungle. She obeyed. After many, many trips she understood the unique beauty of those leaves. She took the leaves back to her room and drew them in her notebook. It *was* art! The jungle was filled with natural art and no one, no matter how talented, could paint or draw as beautifully as the art treasures she found in nature.

Every tree in the jungle was special. According to Khamu belief, a guardian spirit lived inside of each tree, protecting it. When the logging crews came to cut down the trees, this caused great sorrow and anger in the villagers. They grew up with so much respect and love for the trees. When they saw the trees being destroyed, they believed this killed the guardian spirits too. When Lek heard the trees fall, far, far from Baan Lao, she cried.

Trees connected the Khamu with the jungle spirit, almost directly. When a Khamu hill tribe person died, cremation followed. The family chose a tree to hold the ashes. The Khamu believed that a tree held the very soul of a loved one and families looked after the trees that held those souls. Tree cutters were warned not to disturb these sacred resting places. Even though outsiders regarded such beliefs as silly, most were too afraid to cut down the soul-carrying trees.

Hill tribe belief in karma meant that bad deeds in life had to be repaid in death. A bad thing was a much broader idea than committing crimes. The simplest act in life could lead to a debt in death. Eating animal meat, even to survive was considered something a person would have to pay for in death. Lying had to be atoned for in death. Any and all things that violated the law of the jungle, karma demanded them to be answered in death. Trees were the holy vessels that allowed the dead to pay off the debts of karma.

Ghost Creek

Of all the stories that Noom told his granddaughter, none touched her any more deeply, and none frightened her more than a ghost story about a mysterious creek buried deep in the mountain jungle. It was not really a story at all. It was the truth. It was a warning to all villagers and visitors of Baan Lao. Many people heard about Ghost Creek. All of them believed in it. None of them ever dared violate the warning, Noom's warning: *Do not go near this creek during the season of the ghosts!*

It was more than a warning. It was a sacred Khamu vow. Each villager of Baan Lao had to promise never to visit the area of this creek between March and May of each year. Break this promise and a curse would follow. A bad spirit would follow the violator back to the village. This spirit would harm the person's family.

Ghost Creek was locked inside the thickest of jungle forests. It was three mountains away and a hard two-hour walk from Baan Lao. The entire area was a rainforest of tall trees, clusters of bamboo, and rattan vines growing everywhere. The sun could barely penetrate the jungle canopy. To the local Khamu, this was known as the "lost tiger forest." Legend said that even tigers that entered this jungle would lose their way and die in the dense jungle undergrowth.

From the first of March until the end of May, no one was allowed near Ghost Creek except the shaman and the shaman's assistant. This was the season of the ghosts. Ghosts, both the good and bad, gathered at the creek. There they celebrated with bizarre dancing on top of the creek. The fear of actually seeing this terrible dance kept people away. Belief in ghostly spirits who would place a curse on anyone who saw the ghosts dance over the creek, kept everyone away. Men and women from Baan Lao took a sacred oath not to go there during the season of the ghosts. They drank holy water to bind them to this oath.

Grandfather Noom visited Ghost Creek during the forbidden months because it was his duty as shaman. He had to perform certain ceremonies to satisfy the spirit of the jungle. Despite her fears, Lek wanted to go with him. For years he would not even consider it. She was too young, he thought. She was not an assistant shaman and he could not make an exception just because she was his favorite grandchild. Besides, there was a mystery, a secret about Ghost Creek that could not be revealed.

Even though she was not allowed to see Ghost Creek during the forbidden months, Noom began taking her there at other, permitted times. She saw how beautiful it was. A towering waterfall sent crystal clear water down the mountain, cleansing the land, and pouring into the basin below. From there the creek began and ended. Tropical birds played and sang nearby. As the falling water neared the pool at the jungle's bottom, it seemed to turn into a fine mist and a constant fog hovered over the water. To Lek, the vines and trees surrounding the waterfall made this seem like a picture out of a dream, a dream of pure beauty. She could make out the footprints of bears and other animals that had passed through this jungle paradise, stopping to drink from Ghost Creek. It was at the same time a place of indescribable beauty and deep fear for her. It was the fear in knowing this was the very spot where hundreds, perhaps thousands of ghosts came together during their special time.

Lek's curiosity about Ghost Creek grew throughout her childhood. Again and again, she begged her grandfather to take her to the creek. She would risk the curse of the ghosts if she must. Deep down she believed Noom could protect her against the curse. But no matter how many times she asked, and no matter how much she begged, he would not allow her to see the creek, until…

As a young woman, she still had the burning desire to see Ghost Creek during the haunting season. One day Noom surprised her. She could go! She could see the creek during the forbidden time. But before he took her there, he made her promise never to tell anyone in Baan Lao that she went or reveal what she saw. This was not the oath everyone took, bound with holy water. The oath Noom gave her was even stronger. She had to swear on her ancestors' spirits never to tell the villagers. She swore. She knew this was the most sacred promise anyone could make, but she made it.

Noom led her to the mountain that was home to the ghosts. She was familiar with everything including the beautiful waterfall. But before he would let her see the creek on this special journey, he made her close her eyes. This made the walk all the more frightening. It was like walking through a nightmare, helpless to stop the monsters about to attack. She crept through the jungle. As they approached the creek, she heard strange sounds, sounds she was convinced must be the sounds of a thousand dancing ghosts. Her heart was pounding. She knew she was about to come face-to-face with the secret of the creek, so she held her grandfather's hand tightly, bracing herself for the worst.

As she neared the end of the journey, the wind seemed to get stronger. Suddenly the jungle air was filled with the sound of birds and crickets, as if some force was summoning a natural concert. Lek's body was covered in goose bumps. Despite the comforting hand of her grandfather, she was filled with fear and the great expectation so many years of wondering gave her. Then, Noom told her to open her eyes. The time had come. Lek was so deathly scared at this moment, she felt like vomiting.

"I'm scared. I can't. I can't open them, Grandfather."

Noom told her to be brave. She was here to face the secret and she must open her eyes. When she finally did, there they were, thousands of ghosts, dancing a crazy dance just above the water. They were tiny ghosts, black in color, all flitting and darting, jumping and running toward the waterfall. They seemed to be drawn to the water rushing into the creek from above. Then it struck her. They were not ghosts at all. They were bugs. When she got closer she saw exactly what they were. They were shrimp. Thousands of black shrimp were dancing a crazy dance in the creek.

Lek finally learned the secret. After all the years of wondering, the truth was right there in front of her. Noom told her she must always obey the oath she swore and tell no one in the village what she had seen. As the shaman, he had to protect the jungle. He learned about Ghost Creek from another shaman. The decision was made generations ago to protect these special black shrimp from danger. The ghost season was actually the time when the shrimp would swim to the end of the creek, where the water poured down from on high. This is where they laid their eggs. Thousands would seem to dance above the water, looking for dead leaves to deposit their eggs. It took the full three months for the eggs to hatch and the young shrimp to grow large enough to swim downstream. That's why the forbidden time was from March to May. With this legend, shamans protected these special creatures from harm.

Lek watched as the day of the village shaman came to an end. With a little white lie, a tiny creature could be saved from extinction. By the time she dedicated her life to saving elephants from abuse, she saw how good the shamans were. Even if shaman beliefs were strange or different, their work was to listen to nature's call, to nature's needs, which was another way of describing the spirit of the jungle.

Years after she learned the secret of Ghost Creek, Lek saw its destruction. Outsiders with their machines and with their modern knowledge convinced the Khamu to abandon their beliefs in the spirit of the jungle. More and more poachers and hunters entered the jungle around Baan Lao. Animals disappeared, not in the "lost tiger" jungle, but by man. If they were not hunted, they were frightened from their normal habitat by the noise of the gigantic machine called civilization; it pushed them farther and farther away from the land that once fed them. Ghost Creek was no longer protected because very few believed in the legend. Many people went there looking for the shrimp. The shrimp disappeared too. But lessons like this did not leave Lek. She used them to save a much larger creature than a shrimp.

Invasion of the Opium Eaters

The Hmong tribe is one of several northern Thai hill tribes. Originally from the mountainous areas of southern China, the Hmong settled in large numbers in the mountains located near Chiang Mai. They are a proud people with a long and famous history. But one part of that history is not a happy one. Hmong have a history of using opium, a powerful narcotic drug that comes from the poppy plant. Wars have been fought over the drug. Opium smokers become happy and drowsy. Their minds "see" things non-opium users do not. The more opium a person uses, the more the user needs. Opium addiction is strong. Trying to withdraw from long-time opium use is a very painful thing. Lek remembers the Hmong from her childhood. She remembers how opium threatened her village. It was something that upset her entire village.

Grandfather Noom taught her a lot about love. She watched, as year after year, Noom helped the sick get well. She never understood how much respect the people of Baan Lao had for him until one day when Noom began to build a new house for his family. Lek was amazed to see so many turn out to help him. Many were patients of his. Many were not. It seemed that anyone who was able went to help Noom, carrying bamboo, wooden boards, even the grass for the roof. With so many people helping him, it only took him a few days to finish the house.

Noom earned their respect with his good deeds. Everyone knew he would help anyone and never ask for anything in return. The head of the Karen village learned that when Noom spent weeks nursing his son back to health. Even the outsiders, the construction crews, learned of Noom's unlimited kindness. One day one of them got extremely ill from eating poison mushrooms. Noom, who had been mistreated by the same work crew, used his medicine-man powers to cure the man. He did not think of the insults. His only thought was to help someone who needed help. Lek's mother assisted him with the cure.

Her mother—her angel—also taught Lek the importance of giving freely of yourself to help others. Made an orphan by war at the age of two, Phong Sri became one of most caring women in the village. Before both mother and father died, her family owned many acres of farmland and had many rice fields. When her parents died, she was too young to stop land robbers from taking it all. For a while, Phong Sri, her two brothers, and a sister were homeless. All had to work when they were just children. Eventually, other family members took them in.

Because of her difficult childhood, Lek's mother could never go to school. That did not stop her from learning. When her children went to school, Phong Sri would listen as the children recited their lessons at home. She learned to read and write as her oldest child, Boonta, learned. It was a touching sight for Lek, to watch her grown mother "go to school" through her children.

In Baan Lao, large families lived near one another, in areas known as family compounds. They built their bamboo houses close to each other. Lek's family compound included her family plus the families of four uncles. Arguments sometimes broke out between families. But, over the years, the one constant in the compound was Phong Sri. Lek's mother got along with everyone, never argued with anyone, and worked every day to help anyone in the family who needed help.

The love Lek felt coming from her mother and grandfather was just part of the warmth she found in her village. When someone was ill, the entire village knew. The sick person's family received visits from nearly everyone. People brought food to help the family. If someone died, there was crying throughout Baan Lao. Work stopped until the funeral was over. It was as if this tiny mountain town breathed from the same set of lungs, and felt pain and happiness through one large beating village heart. Like closely clustered reeds of bamboo that sway together in the breeze, the entire village was moved when either grief or happiness touched one of their own.

Money did not play a large part in the lives of the villagers. During Lek's childhood, very few people had any. There could be no greed, anger, boasting, or argument over something that no one had. Instead, the villagers used a friendly bartering system, trading rice for fish or meat, or almost any food item for any other food item. If a family ran out of food, other families would bring them what they needed. No one ever went hungry in Baan Lao.

Village life in the 1960s was simple, filled with caring people, and it was Lek's belief that her village was safe. Cows and water buffalo were the beasts of burden. Bamboo pipes carried water from a nearby creek. When it rained, mushrooms sprouted everywhere. The Khamu could survive on a diet of mushrooms, rice, and insects if necessary. People took care of other people. Love was plentiful. Lek may have lived in a tiny hamlet with no electricity and very little sunlight, but her world was far from dark and dismal. Trust in each other was the unspoken rule, understood by all. There was no lying or cheating. If two families had a true disagreement, the shaman was asked to settle matters. There was no stealing. There was nothing that could upset the warm closeness of her village—until the opium eaters arrived.

More and more outsiders came to Lek's village as northern Thailand was "improved" with new roads and power lines. One day, another of the many road crews arrived to construct a new road near the village. At night, the men working on the project would visit Baan Lao. At first, they were welcome. They brought news from the rest of the world, meaning from the rest of Thailand, into the little jungle community. Villagers listened to them give news reports. Before they came, there was a nightly ritual of listening to the government radio station as it broadcast the evening news over the radio. Baan Lao had one battery-powered transistor radio for this nightly event. The storytellers were treated like special guests.

Less than a mile from the village lived several members of the Hmong hill tribe. They lived almost side-by-side with their Khamu neighbors for decades. But their way of life was very different. Hmong men could have more than one wife. When Lek was a child, it was the custom for the men to stay in the house and the women to work in the rice and corn fields. Opium smoking by the men taking care of household chores was common.

The Hmong near Lek's village sold opium to the construction teams in the area. The Hmong grew the poppies, extracted opium from the seedpods, and even built little opium huts used for selling the drug and as a "safe" place for smoking it. The Khamu did not interfere with the affairs of another tribe, but they did not of approve the practice of selling opium either. Because one road crew was working so close to Baan Lao, an opium hut was built there, in the middle of the village. It was less than fifty yards from Lek's house. The Hmong owner thought this would make it more convenient to those of the crew who wished to smoke the powerful drug.

The hut caused a great stir in the village. The villagers grew worried. They could not sleep well. The opium buyers and smokers were too close to their houses, and, perhaps more troublesome, too close to the children of the village including

Lek. The entire village seemed to be under the influence of a curse—an opium curse. Strange things began to happen. Chickens screamed at night.

Lek's parents told her never to go near the place, but her child's curiosity got the better of her. One day she entered the hut. Inside the opium hut she saw a man with a large black ball of opium and a scale. When a customer from the road crew entered, the Hmong seller would mix opium from the black ball with some white powder, weigh it, and sell it to his buyer. Lek noticed that opium users had yellowish skin, perhaps from their constant use of the drug. She watched as opium smokers would lie down on the floor and smoke their drug.

Near the top of the hut, jungle lizards scrambled around. She saw how they seemed to scamper toward the opium smoke as it drifted upwards. Once directly under the smoke, they would lift their tails, seeming to enjoy it. On days when the hut was not open, the lizards fell to the ground and barely moved. Lek asked her grandfather why they acted like that. Noom told her the lizards were addicted to the drug just like the men.

Noom warned the people not to let their children go near the hut. But the Hmong built it very near the place where the children loved to play. It was impossible to avoid it. Noom asked the owner to remove it, tear it down, and build it outside of Baan Lao. He refused. In a very short time, Noom returned. He was not alone. Almost every man in the village went with Noom to the hut. They were armed with arrows, knives, large pieces of wood, and axes. The opium hut was torn down. The owner ran away with his opium and built another hut near a logging camp.

The Buddha Thieves

When the opium hut was taken down, things seemed to return to normal. Baan Lao was once again a peaceful jungle village. Simple things like jungle sights and sounds could be enjoyed. People sat in the evenings on the tiny balconies or the porches of their huts and watched the light show from hundreds of fireflies. Crickets seemed to sing in harmony with jungle frogs. Unfortunately, the calm did not last.

Not long after the opium dealer was forced out of the village, more newcomers arrived. Three men came, they said, to learn about herbal medicine. Shaman Noom liked them instantly. They seemed sincerely interested in learning from a master, from the village shaman. Noom felt honored to have outsiders seek his advice and consider him, as they told him, a great medicine man.

When the three city men first arrived in Baan Lao, Lek and Noom were deep in the jungle, searching for medicinal plants. The men asked Lek's father if they could stay at his house while they studied under Noom. Lek's family was honored to have the guests under their small grass roof. When Lek returned from the jungle, she was surprised to see that her parents had prepared a meal for the three city men. Noom sat proudly eating with the family, answering many questions asked by the guests.

When the dinner was finished, the talk about herbal medicine continued. Noom gave the men one of his special treats, a banana leaf and herb cigarette. Other men from Baan Lao joined them. Everyone was struck by how polite these outsiders were. They told stories that made everyone laugh—everyone except for one small child. Lek had a very bad feeling about them as soon as she began listening to them. Something about them did not seem right. But she could not say anything. That would have been rude.

The second evening with the city visitors seemed like the first. They joined Lek's family for the evening meal. One man took out a notebook and made notes as the three of them asked more questions of Grandfather Noom. The children went to bed as the men talked into the night. That's when it happened. That's when Lek woke up to a nightmare. One of the "nice" men woke her up with his shouts. He was shouting at Lek's mother, Phong Sri. When Lek went to see what was happening, things only got worse. The man stuck a gun in her mother's back and ordered her to place all of the children in one room. Phong Sri begged the man not to harm her children.

The three men rounded up the entire family and put them all in one room. They tied Noom and Lek's parents to a pole. The children were not tied, but were frightened beyond belief. Lek's younger sister, Phan Nee, screamed uncontrollably. This only made the gunmen angry. One of them told Lek's mother to stop the girl from crying or else…he did not say what might happen, but Phong Sri understood more violence could come. No matter how much she begged, Lek's mother could not stop Phan Nee from screaming. At one point, one of the men threw a blanket over her, but that just made her scream more.

It was a shocking scene. The outsiders had come to rob them, not to learn from Noom. Now they were being forced to use their weapons by a little girl's screams. When the blanket did not stop her from screaming, the man with the gun stuck the barrel of the gun in Phan Nee's face, ready to pull the trigger. She continued to scream. With the gun nearly in her mouth, she wailed louder than ever!

The men untied Lek's mother and told her to take care of her daughter. Phong Sri knew things might get much more violent and bloody if she could not stop her daughter from screaming. She went over to the little girl and held her tightly. As soon as she did this, Phan Nee became quiet. All of the children huddled together, shaking in fear.

The three men then made their demands. Where was the money? And where was the figure of Buddha? They were certain that Noom had been paid in silver coins from his days of helping men in the logging camps. They were wrong. There was no such money. They also believed that the shaman must own a very ancient and valuable image of Buddha. In this they were right. Noom guarded his Buddha throughout his lifetime. To him it was priceless. To these thieves it was worth a lot of money.

The three robbers threatened to kill Noom and his family unless he told them where the silver was buried. But no matter how many times they threatened him, Noom gave them the same answer. He told them the truth. There was no silver. The men tore apart Noom's medicine hut. They were certain a treasure was buried there. Noom's precious herbs were thrown everywhere. When it became clear that there was no money, the robbers turned their attention to the figure of Buddha. This did exist. Noom was not willing to risk the lives of his family to hold on to it, despite its great worth.

Once her grandfather gave the Buddha to the men, they left. They left without any money, but more importantly, they left without harming anyone. Lek's father, Sa-Nguan, got loose first and untied the other adults. He ran immediately to the bamboo emergency bell and rang it, alerting the entire village. Soon, Lek saw the men of Baan Lao crowd together, and then leave together.

The three outsiders escaped through the jungle with their stolen Buddha. But they only knew one path through the jungle. It was the long way out. The band of village men knew this. They took a shorter route known only to them. They set up an ambush knowing the three men had to pass them soon. When the robbers ran into their trap, the villagers surrounded them, holding their weapons ready to attack. They forced the three men to return the image of Buddha. Then they told the men to leave and never return. They did not harm them.

Since that day, things changed in Baan Lao. The opium hut was a serious violation of their peace and safety, but the outsiders who tried to rob them and who threatened to shoot innocent people, left the entire village mistrusting outsiders. They placed a lookout near the entrance to the village. When an outsider was seen walking toward the village, the lookout warned the others. Doors were shut. Visitors were no longer welcome. After being alerted, the tiny jungle village looked like a ghost town. It was a very sad thing for Lek to see. It was sad for everyone there.

Master Suwan and His Little Pigs

Not every outsider who came to Baan Lao was bad. One was good. His name was Mr. Suwan. He had served in the Thai military as an instructor. He was a very tough man. He must have scared many young Thai men under his command. When he finished his military service, he became a road builder, using his strict military ways to build many roads for the government. This business brought him to Baan Lao. One day he fell ill and Noom used his skills with herbal healing to cure him. Noom and Mr. Suwan became friends out of this chance "doctor-patient" meeting. From time to time, Mr. Suwan would stay at Lek's family compound. His friendship would eventually help Lek do something very few hill tribe children could do: *succeed at the government school.*

The older she got, Lek's parents grew more and more concerned over her safety. It wasn't the long walk that worried them. More and more outsiders appeared. Lek and her Khamu friends saw more and more men working near the paths they took to school. Even though the robbers and opium smokers were gone, the more Lek began to look like a young woman, the more looks she would get from these men. When she was almost eleven, her parents decided they had to do something to keep her safe from harm.

One day Lek's parents decided to walk with her to school. They told her they would try to find a place close to the school where she could stay during the year. She would no longer have the long walk through the jungle, the walk that gave them more and more concern. Instead, her parents went to the home of Mr. Suwan, the road builder. They asked him if Lek could stay with his family.

Mr. Suwan would not agree unless Lek's parents met his demands. First, they must pay him 150 baht per month. At the time this was roughly equal to six U.S. dollars. Though it may not have seemed like much, to hill tribe villagers it was a lot of money. This would help pay Lek's room and meals at Mr. Suwan's house. Next, her parents had to agree to let Lek work for Mr. and Mrs. Suwan. She would have to clean the house and wash their clothes. She would also have to cut the wheat and grass, and make sure the outside yard always looked neat and clean.

Mr. Suwan and his wife lived in a large, two-story teakwood house. On the first floor was the family store. It was the only store in the area, making it very popular. It offered everything from food items to farm products including chemical fertilizers, and even construction crew clothes and tools.

Lek did not mind working for her room and board. She was raised to work hard, just like all Khamu children. From the age of six she went with her parents when they planted rice or corn. By eight her mother was teaching her how to cook. As the first daughter in the family, it was her job to learn all of the chores that had to be done to take care of the entire household. Many times it was Lek who watched over her younger brother and four younger sisters. So Mr. Suwan's work requirements did not stop

Lek's mother and father from letting her stay there. In fact, Mr. Suwan agreed to take in both Lek and her brother, Boonta, as school-year boarders.

There was one more thing Mr. Suwan insisted upon. It was something that would help Lek survive during her separation from her parents. Lek would have to take care of the farm animals. Of all of the things she would miss from Baan Lao, it was her animals. The little doctor always had a small crowd of animals living in her room and in the compound. Fortunately, Mr. Suwan had many animals to care for. Lek happily accepted the job.

When the people of Baan Lao heard that two of Phong Sri's children would be staying with the Suwans, jealousy broke out. More families wanted the same thing. Soon, Mr. Suwan agreed to let four more hill tribe kids join Lek and her brother at the house. All of them shared a large room on the second floor of the house. All of them had chores to do. Now Mr. Suwan had a little hill tribe army working for him.

The ex-soldier and former military trainer never lost his military ways. Mr. Suwan was always tough, even toward the children. All of his little soldiers had to follow his strict orders. The six students even had to learn how to walk in the house. This meant learning to walk so no one else could hear, just as a soldier must walk so that the enemy could not hear. Lek and Boonta, and the four other Khamu children walked on their tiptoes. If Mr. Suwan detected one of them, the violator of the noise rule would receive a sharp smack with a bamboo stick.

When he was a military instructor for brand new Thai recruits, every morning and every night was the same. Recruits got up early, well before the sun rose, and went to sleep at the exact same hour, the "lights out" hour. There were no exceptions. Mr. Suwan's little army of six did exactly the same. They were up each day by 4:30. After finishing their morning exercise, into a cold shower they went, one by one. It did not matter what season, or how cool the morning breeze was, the morning routine never changed.

The rules for the evening were as unbendable. Once they finished their jobs around the house, the evening was spent studying. Before they went to sleep, they had to do two things without fail. First, they had to pledge their loyalty to their king and country. Just before lights out, they had to say a prayer to Buddha.

The Khamu children dared not disobey Mr. Suwan's rules. To violate them meant the bamboo stick would come out. When a student did not wake up on time, the bamboo rod would find its way on the young child's legs. Mr. Suwan would continue to strike, although not very hard, until his little soldier was out of bed. All of this discipline had a purpose, at least to the ex-soldier. The children did not understand it at the time. It took Lek several years to see that Mr. Suwan and his strange ways made her strong. He trained her and the others in combat. He taught them to fight in war. But it was not a war against an enemy holding a gun. It was a much more cunning enemy. It was against the enemy of prejudice. It was a war between the hill tribe peoples of Thailand and all the rest.

The prejudice was strong, and, to Lek, it seemed to be everywhere she went. It was not unusual for her to hear that something was "as stupid as a Khamu," or "dirty like a Khamu." Mr. Suwan was preparing his young soldiers to stand up and be proud. Yes, they were hill tribe kids. Yes, hill tribe people were looked down upon. But, under his roof, no one was allowed to use bad language. No one could be lazy. There would be no one caught picking his nose or spitting. He trained them not to do anything that would give outsiders a reason for making fun of them.

Mr. Suwan was always very blunt. He said what he meant and he meant what he said. There was no gentleness about the way he acted or spoke. Things in his world were black or white, good or bad, right or wrong. He didn't bother with the hard, in-between grays or the indecisive partial rights and wrongs. When he explained something to his little boarders, he used simple, even strange examples. There were two things a student staying in his house must never be: a cow or a slave. Cows, he told them, cared about just one thing: eating grass. Slaves were even worse because they lived to be free of their work, and there were only two times when this happened, when they ate and when they slept. This really did not make much sense, but Mr. Suwan believed it completely. The children had no choice; they believed

The Elephant Lady of Thailand

it because he told them to. In any event, if he caught them acting like a slave or a cow, bad things would happen.

Cows and slaves may think about eating, but to Mr. Suwan eating was something no child should ever abuse. Wasting food was one of the big crimes in the Suwan house. One day Mr. Suwan inspected his troops as they ate their evening meal. He saw that some children had let a few grains of their rice fall to the floor. He handed a large bamboo basket to one of the children who let the rice grains fall from his plate. He told him to pick up the three or four tiny grains of rice and place them in the huge basket. He then ordered all six children outside where he led them on ten trips around the house. As they walked, he had them repeat after him:

Thank you to the farmer,
We appreciate your hard work in growing rice for us to eat,
We are sorry we threw rice and wasted it on the floor,
We know that isn't right,
We know you have shown us so much kindness with your work,
We will never throw our rice again.

After that day, there was never another time when even a single grain of rice fell to the floor.

Mr. Suwan told his boarders that their job was to do well in school. They would work hard to finish their daily chores, and then study each evening before lights out. This did not leave much time for playing. That is exactly how Mr. Suwan wanted it. Over time, Lek realized that her master's plan really worked. Each of the six Khamu boarders earned among the highest grades of their class. Though they all walked in fear around Mr. Suwan, when they received a high grade, they forgot that fear and eagerly went to show him.

The Khamu children were not the only ones under the spell of Mr. Suwan. When they went to the government school before they lived at his house, they were treated very badly. Just as Lek had learned, even the teachers treated the Khamu badly. When fights broke out between Khamu students and the others, teachers sided with the others. Khamu students sat in the worst of chairs at broken-down tables. But when word spread that six were under the Suwan roof, it was as if Mr. Suwan snapped his fingers and the teachers changed their ways instantly. SNAP! Lek, Boonta, and the other Khamu kids sat at a new table in the classroom on chairs that were not ready to fall apart. SNAP! They may not have been treated well, but a teacher was never caught actually mistreating them. SNAP! Students who used to pick on the Khamu now kept their distance. Why the Khamu army was treated better is not clear. It may have been because of Mr. Suwan's military ways. It may have been because everyone in the area needed what he sold in his store. But, no matter what the reason, the Khamu enjoyed being under the protective spell of their master.

Even though the children lived in fear of Mr. Suwan, they loved and adored his wife. "Mom Phen," as they called her, was the exact opposite of their military master. Mr. and Mrs. Suwan never had children, so Mom Phen treated the Khamu boarders as her own. Her husband warned her not to spoil them, but she was always taking extra food to them when he was not looking.

For Lek, there was only one other thing besides Mom Phen that helped her survive her separation from her family and from her beloved animals. It was her other job at the Suwan house, taking care of the farm animals, that became her lifeline. In particular, she loved taking care of the pigs. Each morning before school, she fed them. In a very short time they could tell that Lek loved them. When she got near them they would cry to her, craning their heads toward her, squealing for her attention. She loved to spend time with them, sometimes stopping to rub their bellies. She even named them and they all seemed to answer to their names. Mr. Suwan's neighbors looked at Lek in disbelief when they heard her "talking" to her little piggies.

One day, when Lek was far from her pigs, she heard them screaming for dear life. She had never heard such painful screams from them. She ran as fast as she could. When she got to the pigs she saw them all tied up, thrown in the back of a pickup truck. Mr. Suwan had sold them to a butcher and they were going to be killed. When she realized what was happening, tears poured down Lek's cheeks. She climbed into the pickup truck and tried to comfort her little pigs. She rubbed their stomachs so they would fall asleep. She saw the truck driver give Mr. Suwan

The Elephant Lady of Thailand

some money. After a while, they chased her away from the truck. Her pigs were driven away, again screaming as loudly as when she first heard them. Lek could not sleep that night. The sound of their cries stayed with her for many years. The noise was like a sharp knife cutting her heart. Things would only get worse.

Lek's time at the Suwan house went by until the day came when it was time to go to another government school, a high school located in another city. Thanks to Master Suwan she did very well in school. Thanks to him, she learned lessons in and out of the classroom. Her older brother, Boonta, left the Suwan home ahead of her. During the last months of Lek's stay, Mom Phen was ill. She grew to depend on Lek more and more since Lek was the only girl left at the house. Mrs. Suwan needed her to take care of the house as well as to help run the store. Mr. Suwan was away building roads. Lek could not refuse and this made her homesickness for her jungle village even worse. When she was finally able to go back for a visit, Grandfather Noom looked very old and weak. Lek's father now collected herbs for him from the jungle. Both Mrs. Suwan and Noom were slipping away.

Caring for Mom Phen became more and more difficult. She called Lek into her room one night and Lek could not believe how weak she looked. She tried to give her some food to make her stronger, but Mom Phen would only take water. Lek was so scared she ran to the neighbor's house. When they returned, the neighbor tried to talk Mom Phen into going to the hospital, but she refused. Lek continued to watch over her. Later that night she saw that Mrs. Suwan must have suffered a stroke. She lay in bed not moving at all and her eyes were wide open. Lek ran through a monsoon shower to get the neighbor again. They took Mom Phen to the hospital. Two days later, the next time Lek saw her, she was in a coffin.

In just a short time, Lek felt the pain of many losses. She lost her little piggies. Her brother left. Her beloved grandfather was not the same man she grew up with. Mrs. Suwan died. Her father wanted her to return to Baan Lao after Mom Phen died. She did for a while. But she could not stay away for long. She remembered how Master Suwan cried when his wife passed away. He had always been so tough, but now he was just like everyone else. She knew he needed help. Lek returned to the

Suwan house and helped him clean it. She did everything she could to help him. It was not the same and she knew it never would be.

The Price of Life

The government school near the Suwan house took Lek into her teen years. She finished her studies there one year after brother Boonta left. The next step, and it was a very big step, was to prepare for Thai high school. For that she had to attend pre-high school studies devoted to getting her ready for the last part of a government education. The closest school for this was located in another city and far from her jungle home. To get there it wasn't the distance that was the problem; it was her father.

Sa-Nguan, Lek's father, wanted her to end her school studies. She already had more education than most Khamu children, and certainly more than most girls. He felt it was time for her to take care of their house. He worried that going to school in the big city would change her forever, and remove the Khamu ways from her spirit. He and Phong Sri fought over the subject.

Khamu belief was at the heart of the argument. Spirits could not be insulted. The Khamu believe that when a girl becomes a woman, she must present herself to a man untouched by any other man. If she cannot, she insults the spirits of her ancestors. One evening after dinner, the argument heated up and finally exploded once and for all. Her parents spent several hours talking about it. Phong Sri insisted that she could control her daughter. She said she would make Lek promise to stay away from boys and never do anything to lose her honor. She would vow never to violate the sacred belief that she must remain pure until marriage. But Sa-Nguan, Lek's father, did not believe it. His greatest fear was that Lek would go off to the big city and become pregnant.

For a while there was a standoff between Lek's mother and father. But Lek had one more, very powerful person on her side: Noom. Her grandfather also supported her desire to continue her education. In the end, after hours of arguing, Lek's father finally agreed to let her go. On the morning when they told her, she had to listen to her mother and agree to keep the promises her father insisted she make.

Lek's first trip to the big city where she would attend the school was not a good one. She rode on the back of a logging truck with her mother. She was sick the whole way, vomiting several times. When they arrived, things only got worse. The smell of the city, its pollution and market smells, made it hard for her to even breathe. Everywhere she went, the traffic and people created a thundering noise in her head. She was more frightened here than on her first trip to see Ghost Creek during the forbidden time. The people were so different than the villagers of Baan Lao. They were so loud. Some swore in anger. She saw others fighting. After just her first day in the city, Lek wanted to leave and never return. But she did not. Becoming an educated Khamu woman was more important. To her, this was the most important thing in her life.

It was decided that Lek would stay with her aunt, her mother's sister, who everyone called Miss Nang. She had never married and welcomed the company of her niece. Miss Nang agreed to help Lek pay the various school fees in return for Lek's help with her business. Her aunt sold tobacco and tea in the local market. Lek would wake up hours before school and help her aunt take the products to her market stall. Miss Nang also allowed Lek to have pets and care for stray cats. Lek was very happy living with her. The school was only a short distance from her aunt's house.

Once she got used to the noise, the smells, and the fast pace of the city, Lek settled down to just learning. She still missed the village and everything in it. The homesickness was just as bad as when she lived with Master Suwan and his wife. She made few trips home because they were just too difficult. Her mother worried terribly each time she did. To get back to the jungle from the city, she began with a long ride on a public bus. Then she had to make a connection and transfer to a local bus. After that, she had to find a ride on a logging truck. If she got lucky, a typical truck ride would leave her just a three-mile walk to the village.

Lek's mother did not want her returning home unless it was absolutely necessary. The long trip home and the connections she had to make were too much for Phong Sri. It was left up to Lek's aunt to decide if she could go home. But one day the trip had to be made. It was absolutely necessary. Grandfather Noom was sick. Miss Nang gave her permission to go.

Lek rode the buses without any problem. She made her connection. But when she found a logging truck, the driver told her she must pay for a seat on his truck. She hadn't counted on this, but she gladly agreed because this truck would pass right by Baan Lao. Lek joined a group of about fifteen men and women who were heading to the logging camp to work.

As the youngest and smallest, Lek was told that she must sit up front and stay out of the way. Seated between the driver and his assistant, she saw a large pile of chains on the floor. They would be used to bind the logs to the truck. The old truck creaked and moaned as they rode along the dirt road toward the village. It was the rainy season and the road had been turned into a thick and slippery muddy mess from recent rains. Driving up and down this road was slow going and extremely dangerous. The truck would get stuck in the mud. The driver's assistant would then jump out and place a large, wedge-shaped block of wood next to one of the rear tires, in front of it when the truck headed downhill, or behind it if the truck was climbing a hill. All of the passengers were ordered out and converted into a work crew to pull or push the truck out of the mud. Lek was not allowed to leave the front seat. The driver thought she was too small to be of any use.

The truck continued on. Many times it got stuck. Many times Lek watched from her seat as the driver and his assistant gave directions to fifteen straining passengers. As the driver was trying to get down a very steep hill, it became harder and harder to control the big rig. The truck kept sliding in one direction and then another. One wrong move and it would slide right off the mountain. Unable to control it any more, he stopped about halfway down the hill. He ordered his assistant to place the wooden block at the front tire so he could check the road that lay ahead. Everyone got out as he did this—everyone except for Lek.

Suddenly, the truck jumped the wooden block and started sliding down the mountain, out of control, wildly careening from side to side. Lek screamed for help but it was too late. The truck left the others standing in the mud, staring in amazement after it. She heard the onlookers shouting after her. The next sounds she heard were the sounds of the run-away truck crashing against trees and huge rocks as it half-slid and half-rolled down the hill. The collisions sounded like great claps of thunder. Her tiny body was tossed around in the cab of the truck. After several violent clashes between the truck and the side of the mountain, something grabbed her, choking the air out of her. It was the giant set of logging chains. She had become entangled in the big pile as the truck rattled down the mountain.

Lek's wild ride came to a sudden stop. The truck struck something hard and slid no further. The thunderous noise was replaced with dead silence and darkness. Lek lay inside the truck in great pain. The logging chains were completely wrapped around her. She couldn't move. She didn't know where the truck had come to rest. She had no idea if it would start to slide again. The air seemed thin to her. Breathing was difficult. She had never been so scared. She heard voices from above. They seemed far, far away.

One of the distant voices was from a man who swore and said, "I think she's dead!" Lek wanted to shout up with all her might that she was NOT dead. She was alive. She needed help! Please come now! Help her get out of the truck! Help free her from the prison of heavy chains! But Lek could only *think* of what she wanted to scream. For some reason, she could not speak. She was trapped inside the steel cage of the truck's cab, and wrapped in logging chains. Her throat seemed to be paralyzed.

She heard more voices, but now they seemed to be much nearer. "Do you know who she is?" one man asked. The answer would prove much more painful than all of the pain caused by the truck's slide down the mountain: "Don't worry. She's just a Khamu." They were unforgettable words. They told her that she, the little doctor who loved all creatures, did not count for much among human creatures. If she died in a terrible accident, it was okay because she was "just a Khamu."

The voices seemed very close now. She heard the next one: "Pay her parents a thousand baht, maybe two. They will jump at it." Now she had a value. But it wasn't the kind she wanted. A man had just announced that a small amount of money would solve the problem of her dying in a truck accident. Two thousand baht or less than fifty U.S. dollars would buy her parents' silence. There would be no investigation. There would be no trouble.

It was a nightmare for Lek. Now the voices seemed to be right outside of her steel prison. She listened to them, unable to do anything to save herself. They seemed to talk for a very long time. It was all about what to do with the dead Khamu girl. The chain weighted her down so it was difficult to move at all. The driver and his assistant must have been peering inside by now, seeing her wrapped in the chain's death grip, and believing she really was dead. She must be dead. She did not move. The truck was wrecked. The chain had crushed her to death.

At some point Lek felt she really was going to die unless she moved something. She pushed with one hand against the chains. She pushed with all of the strength she could find. Someone saw her hand move. A voice said, "Look! Her hand moved! She's alive!" Then some men rushed over and pulled the chains off of Lek. A man lifted her from the truck. Lek felt a rush of air hit her and make her dizzy. She began to throw up.

The Death of Two Giants

Lek was growing up. She was still a girl, but fast becoming a young woman. She was learning about life through all she did. Her life experiences made her strong. She knew what it was to be from a people that other people of the same country regarded as inferior. This only fed her desire to show everyone that a tiny hill tribe girl could do much in her world. Her childhood in the jungle nourished her love for all creatures great and small. Grandfather Noom taught her that all living things meant something. No life form, no matter how meaningless it seemed to others, was without meaning and purpose on this earth. Whether it was "ghost shrimp" dancing in a creek, or lizards being abused by opium eaters, or the many plants and trees at the mercy of all, or the jungle's most magnificent creations, her beloved elephants, they all had a purpose. They all had meaning in this jungle world. So it was very painful for Lek to watch the man who taught her so much about life begin to lose his grip on his own life.

As he neared the end, Noom tried to warn his granddaughter. The jungle was fast disappearing. She must do something, even if only a small thing, to show the mountain spirit and the jungle spirit, that she knew about this threat. So many people were entering the jungle and causing damage. It was damage done by the outsiders but now even the villagers of Baan Lao violated the rules. If they saw how effective a certain jungle herb was as medicine, they would go into the jungle to find the plant containing the leaves. Instead of taking just what they needed, or instead of removing leaves in a way that did no harm to the plant, they would pull out the entire plant. Sometimes they would cut away all the leaves and the plant would die. Noom worried that such waste was destroying many jungle cures and people were insulting the Great Spirit.

Noom and Lek took only what they needed. Noom was always careful to show his respect to the spirit of the jungle in all he did. When he and Lek would take their lunch in the jungle, they would place a small amount of the food they brought on a nearby plant. This was to thank the spirit and to apologize for any damage done by their visit. Noom taught her that nothing was really free in the jungle. If you took something, you had to leave something. All of life was a system of constant trades: this for that; food for leaves; herbal cures for humans meant that humans must restore the herbs they took. To keep a balance, and let nature prosper, Noom insisted that everyone live as a trader.

Lek was born to respect the jungle. She was so different than the rest of her family, especially her father, Sa-Nguan. Lek could not bring herself to kill a wild animal, even though hunting was necessary to put food on the family table. Her brother, Boonta, and her sisters loved to go with their father to kill game. It was expected of Khamu fathers to teach their children how to survive through hunting. But Lek wanted no part of it and one hunting trip told her father she was terribly different.

Sa-Nguan planned a bird-hunting trip. He would take Lek and her sisters to help him. Lek watched him prepare the "traps." First he collected sap from rubber trees and boiled it until it turned into a very sticky paste. This was applied to several tree branches. Rice and seeds were sprinkled onto the branches. When they got to the bird-hunting, or rather bird-trapping area, near a stream in the jungle, Sa-Nguan would spread these branches around the banks of the creek. When birds flew in to eat the seeds and rice, their feet stuck to the branches and the branches weighed them down so they could not fly. It was so simple and to Lek, so cruel!

Lek and her sister, Phan Nee, were told to watch one end of the creek. Her father and another sister watched the other end. Lek saw several birds fall into the trap. She was horrified to see so many stuck to the branches. Some tried to flap their wings and this only got some of the sap glue stuck in their feathers. She saw the frightened look in their little eyes. She couldn't let them die. Her sister watched in amazement as Lek freed most of the birds. One fought so hard to get loose that it was near death when Lek arrived. When the two sisters met their father on the other end of the creek, Phan Nee immediately told on her sister. Sa-Nguan was angry beyond belief. He shouted at Lek for several minutes. He told her she could not eat that evening, but her mother found a way to take her food. It was clear to everyone that Lek was different—terribly different.

The jungle may look open to all. It might seem to be a place filled with free plants and animals for the taking. It is not. There is a force that owns it. The mountain spirit owns it. The jungle spirit owns it. Those who enter thinking it is not owned, that they may do as they wish, will only harm it. They do not understand that to take something away means to lose part of the whole. As his own life began to slip away, Noom was most concerned about this, about the destruction of the world around him. He told Lek that each time a person damaged the jungle, if the damage could not be repaired, that person must offer a prayer of apology. Whether ants were killed by someone's footsteps, or small trees were crushed, the violator must ask forgiveness from the spirit.

The days Lek spent with Noom in his last moments were some of the most precious hours of her young life. At times, when Noom appeared especially frail, it seemed as if Lek was the teacher. Because Noom never left the jungle, he wondered about that "other world," the one outside of Baan Lao that Lek had visited many times. In his lifetime the village never had electric power.

"But how does it work?" he would ask. Lek would explain.

"How does it make light?" Lek would try to explain.

"Where does the light come from?" Lek would do the best she could.

When she told him whole cities were lit up at night, he would ask her to describe exactly how one would look.

One day Lek noticed her grandfather looked especially sad and very weak. He surprised Lek when he asked her if she would carry on, if she would continue the tradition of using herbal medicines to cure the local people. The way he looked and the way he asked, it told her that he meant *after he was gone*. Noom's sadness came from thoughts of the new day and of a dark era in the region. Loggers had come and the beautiful peacefulness of Noom's special world was disappearing. Roads were being built all around the area. Roads meant progress and progress meant, well, it meant more noise and more people. Noise disturbed the jungle calm. It changed the natural songs that echoed from gibbons and birds. Progress was destroying much of what Noom loved the most. Lek could see it in his face. It was the look of fear. Noom looked longingly at the mountain beyond as he told her that it was all changing. Hornbill birds were almost gone from the area because poachers hunted them to sell in the market.

This time Noom seemed defeated. His voice was weak as he spoke to her. She did not know what to say to him. She had no idea if she had the strength to continue his work. How could she, a Khamu girl, stand up against the forces that threatened the area? All she could tell him to comfort him was the truth. One of her last promises to her grandfather was that she would always try to be a good person. She also promised that she would study hard and make everyone proud of her. Lek took his hand. She knew it was time to say goodbye. She hugged him tightly.

Three days later one of her cousins came to her house in the family compound with the news. Grandfather Noom had passed away. He died in his medicine hut, still working with his herbs. The shaman of Baan Lao was dead. The village leader was dead. The medicine man was dead. The protector of the surrounding jungle was dead. To Lek, her beloved grandfather was dead. Years earlier the tiny moonlight girl was in awe over the number of people who came to help Noom rebuild his house. Now, much older, Lek again was struck by the huge throngs of people coming to such a tiny jungle village as Baan Lao. They came from all over the region, all to pay their final respects to Noom. Lek's mother gathered up the remaining herbal medicine that Noom had prepared. She handed out little packets of the medicine to the guests attending the funeral ceremony. Nothing that Noom ever did in his life was wasted. The last remains of his work after he died must also be put to good use.

When the funeral was over, the family discussed where to put the ashes of Noom. Lek was given the honor of selecting the tree where the ashes would reside. It was not a difficult decision. On one of their many walks through the jungle Noom told her which tree he loved the most. It was the banyan tree. Banyan trees are extremely hardy with roots that literally claim the surrounding jungle. The banyan has always held a special place of honor in Asian folklore, often symbolizing eternal life. It was no wonder that Noom picked this for his final resting place. In a tree that spread its roots deep into the jungle he loved, his spirit could live forever!

Not long after Noom's death, Lek returned to the jungle. It was very different making such a visit without him. It felt so strange, sensing his presence and yet hurting over his absence. The jungle itself seemed strange. On this, her first trip since Noom's death, everything seemed so quiet. There was no song of nature at all. She stopped at the banyan tree and prayed for her grandfather. She spoke to his spirit, promising that she would always take care of his tree. In the years that followed, Lek would stop and offer food to his spirit. It became a solemn ritual. The banyan tree was her own little temple. It received her secrets. The tree was her medium, her channel to Grandfather Noom. She would stop and talk to him, telling him about problems and challenges that she faced. Sometimes she would proudly tell him about a great victory at school. To her, these were not one-sided little talks. There was someone or something there to receive her thoughts—a memory—a spirit—a kind teacher. In her heart, he never died.

A year passed since Noom's death. The sprawling banyan tree safely guarded his ashes. He was part of the jungle he loved so much. In Noom's little northern Thai kingdom, another great figure came to rest. Chang Thongkam lay down in the jungle to sleep. Sa-Nguan found her. She was dead. The Golden Elephant had joined Noom in the jungle in permanent sleep. Both had given so much to the people. Now the jungle reclaimed them. They were now two happy spirits that floated through the jungle forest forever.

Noom was known throughout the region, in and around Baan Lao, and in Karen villages that he visited to cure a sick animal or child, or to perform a shaman ceremony. There are still tracts of jungle near Baan Lao that no companies will develop because of Noom. They are to remain pristine in his honor. There are no signs saying this. There are no laws requiring it. But everyone in the region feels something very powerful: *the spirit of Noom wills it.*

It was no wonder that Noom picked this for his final resting place. In a tree that spread its roots deep into the jungle he loved, his spirit could live forever! [This is the banyan tree in Baan Lao where Noom's ashes reside.]

Pang Boon Ma: Eyes without a Soul

Lek lived with Miss Nang until she finished high school. Now more than anything else she wanted to go to college, and attend the university in Chiang Mai. But she could not remain at Miss Nang's. That would mean a two-hour bus ride one way. Instead, Lek learned of a missionary group very near the university that welcomed hill tribe people. It was a Christian group and this immediately caused problems with her father. Just as Sa-Nguan was concerned that living in the city to attend school would change Lek, her father feared that the Christian missionaries would destroy her Khamu beliefs.

Those beliefs were sacred to Khamu families. Outsiders describe them with the term animism. This is belief not in a religion so much as belief in the spirits of nature and in the presence of a soul in all things living and nonliving. No matter how Lek's Khamu beliefs are described by others, those beliefs bind a Khamu family together. Lek's father worried that if Lek lived among Christian missionaries, he would lose his daughter to them. Lek was now old enough to deal with her father. It was her decision to go to college and this meant that it was necessary to live with the missionaries. She promised her father that no one would change her and nothing would destroy the Khamu in her. When the missionaries accepted her, she had to abide by their rules. This was not hard for someone who once lived under Master Suwan's roof. But, instead of a prayer to Buddha, the missionaries required prayers to Jesus. Little did Lek know that it would be her Christian friends who would lead her to her life's passion.

It was almost by accident that she found a way to pursue this passion of saving elephants. It happened during lunchtime, when missionaries and hill tribe guests shared a Christian meal together. Lek overheard a group of missionaries talking about a logging camp. The camp was near the border between Thailand and Burma. Their talk turned to a Karen village that needed help. And, most interesting to Lek, they spoke of the many elephants in the area. Some Karen families kept up to fifty elephants in the nearby jungle. Lek asked to join their conversation. When she found out that they would be going to the Karen village with medicine, she asked to go along.

The Elephant Lady of Thailand

They accepted her into their group. The trip was planned for October, when university classes were out for a long holiday. Lek packed her rucksack with medicine that Noom taught her would help sick and injured elephants. The road to the village was even more difficult than the one that led to Baan Lao. When they arrived, there was an immediate problem: the Karen there did not speak Thai. If that was not bad enough, Lek never saw such a poor village. They had no clinic. Medicine was completely absent. They had no school. The sick had no way to leave for an outside hospital. Of course, no one had money.

The Karen villagers were so grateful for the help. But Lek was a complete mystery to them. When she told them that she too was from a hill tribe, they did not believe her. Some laughed when she told them. She had too much knowledge, too much education to be hill tribe. For someone so small to come and help people so poor made some wonder if she was more spirit than human. The morning after the group arrived, Lek showed the Karen that she was what she said she was. She walked into the jungle with the family members of a sick Karen villager. She carefully picked the plants for the herbal cure. As she boiled the herbs and prepared the medicine, she told the family about her training under Shaman Noom. She also told them about Khamu traditions and practices. They soon saw that the Karen and Khamu were not so different. Lek was quickly accepted by the village as a savior. They begged her to return.

In Lek's time, the Karen tribe of northern Thailand was the main tribe that supplied the logging camps with mahouts to control the elephants. In those days there were two types of logging camps. The first was a permanent or long-term camp built close to a good road. This camp would be the central point to receive logs from the other camps. Temporary logging camps were set up where trees could be cut until the supply was gone. Teak groves especially led to temporary camps since the teak tree was highly prized. Furniture made from teak wood was especially profitable. Logs collected at the temporary camp were taken to the permanent camp, loaded onto trucks, and transported to various cities in Thailand.

Lek saw firsthand how elephants were forced to work in the camps. It was a sight that changed her life. It was a horror, second only to phaajaan, the practice of beating and torturing elephants until they obeyed their masters. What Lek saw in the Karen village was not phaajaan, but it was still cruelty practiced on the elephants used to move logs.

Elephants were the chosen beasts of labor in the logging camps. Each elephant moved the cut timber, the heavy logs that only they could move with the brute strength that comes from such a massive body. Karen mahouts guided the elephants. In fact, most of the time a pair of mahouts controlled each elephant. One mahout controlled the elephant's neck and upper movements; the second mahout controlled the legs. Control is not really the way to describe what they did to the elephant to move the heavy logs. A large rope was placed around the elephant's neck, connecting the elephant to the log or logs that must be moved. Over time, this rope cut into the elephant's skin. No matter how much blood, and no matter how terrible were the screams coming from an animal in pain, the work must go on.

The pain inflicted on the elephants was more than the pain of rope burns. Logging in the jungle forest was filled with opportunities for injury. Poorly cut trees had to be yanked out of tight spots yielding skin cuts and body bruises. Uneven ground meant that some loads were being pulled across thickets and rocks that grabbed the load, straining muscles and organs. Sometimes logs rolled down the hillside, or into a creek. The mahouts were expert in prodding their elephants. The upper mahout jabbed the elephant in the head with a large hook. The leg mahout used a knife to persuade the elephant to keep moving its legs. No matter how difficult the job was, elephants were beaten into completing each task. Lek grew sick watching the elephants being tortured this way. It was no wonder that so many of the animals in the logging camps seemed so thin and underweight.

It was when she watched one tortured creature in particular that Lek's plan began to form in her mind. She saw an elephant struggling to do what her mahouts told her to do. She learned that the name of the beautiful creature was Pang Boon Ma. Lek immediately saw that something was very wrong. Pang Boon Ma screamed in pain every time her mahouts made her drag the logs. Little streams of tears trickled down her face. She had a large open cut where the rope around her chest tightened each time she pulled logs. She was crying out in agony because the pain of the rope against her raw skin, rubbing against the open sore was so great. When Lek examined the cut, she saw that the entire area was infected. The wound was filled with pus. She saw tears coming from Pang Boon Ma's beautiful eyes. When she looked into those eyes, all she saw was a hollow stare. The work with all the pain was choking the life spirit from the elephant's soul.

When Lek returned from the trip to the Karen village, the memory of Pang Boon Ma and the pain she suffered in the camp haunted Lek. The tears of the elephant became Lek's own tears, as she thought about the poor, tortured animal. For weeks afterwards all she could do was think of how she must return to the village and help Pang Boon Ma. But to do that, she had to find a way to earn money. She would earn money any way she could. She did not care how. She only wanted the means to buy enough supplies so she could return.

Her first job was working in a restaurant. This provided her just enough money to buy medicine and fill her rucksack for trips back to the elephants. The restaurant owner also allowed her to take leftover food home with her, saving her even more money, which could go to her new mission of mercy. Now she was studying at the university, working at night, and making elephant relief trips into the jungle every chance she could. After returning and treating Pang Boon Ma, she made more and more trips deep into the jungle. With each one she heard of other elephants in need. Her desire to help just one expanded into a mission to treat as many elephants as she could. When the missionary group did not go where elephants were, Lek stopped going with them. She made the jungle trips alone. She was now fully dedicated to the work. Pang Boon Ma and her soulless eyes had changed her life.

You have to see an elephant chained to do logging to understand how painful this can be to the animal. The highly addictive amphetamine, yaba, which means "madness medicine," is used to keep the elephants working around the clock. [Logging is illegal in Thailand but still goes on in nearby countries and still requires the use of elephants.]

Secrets Held by the Jungle

Lek's family went in different directions. Her older brother, Boonta, grew into a rebellious teenager, showing signs that the city had changed him. He was less patient with his family when back in Baan Lao. He brought back new things with him. In her childhood, Lek recalled one transistor radio for the entire village. Boonta now had his very own. For a while, it seemed like Boonta would break away from the family. But not only did Boonta grow out of this phase, he did something remarkable. He finished teachers college. He was the first in the family to become a government official, a teacher assigned to a school located near the Thai-Burma border. He was also the first Khamu member in the entire area to obtain such a job. His family was so proud of him. On the morning when he was to leave for his new assignment, Phong Sri performed a special ceremony in his honor. She took flowers, food, and hot tea to the banyan tree that held Noom's ashes. She made a special prayer to Noom's spirit, asking it to watch over Boonta as he began his new job.

Lek's younger brother, Preecha, was of high school age. Lek worried about him. She wanted him to follow her to high school, living as she did with Miss Nang. But there was no money to pay for his school fees. Lek offered to send some of the money she earned to Miss Nang. With this help, Preecha would also continue his education.

Younger sister, Phan Nee, had a more difficult path to an education. She never went to school as a young girl. By the time she was grown, the only hope for her was a special government school for adults. Sa-Nguan did not want her to leave the village just to attend school. But he listened to Lek, the college student that she was now. More and more, the family followed Lek's advice. Phan Nee eventually attended the school for adults.

By the time Lek entered her college studies, Baan Lao itself had taken a different direction. It was no longer an isolated Khamu jungle village. The government built a good road connecting the area with the larger cities. The village had a new school making the long walks unnecessary. Some new businesses appeared. Cinnamon and sandalwood bark were in demand from spice makers. The once-hidden village was coming under the influence of progress and money.

Lek settled into life as a college student, wishing more than anything to become a veterinarian. No such course of study existed at the university. There was a program that focused on farming and farm animals, but only men were admitted. She became a library science major, something that suited her well, given her love of books and learning. But adjusting to university life was not easy, especially for a Thai woman, and especially for a hill tribe woman at that. During her entire first year of studies, Lek did not return to Baan Lao. She had reached the highest educational level of any Khamu woman and she did not want to risk failing by going home. Besides, her life was now filled with responsibilities. She worked, she studied, and she spent all of her spare time buried deep in the jungle helping elephants.

Unfortunately, Lek found that she could not earn enough money at the restaurant to pay for her trips. As a rescue team of one, it was costly considering she had to pay for transportation, the medicine, and all of the other required supplies. She decided to look for another job through the university's employment office, an office devoted to assisting poor students find work so they could stay in school. Lek got a job with a French company conducting marketing research in Chiang Mai. She took company questionnaires door-to-door. For each questionnaire she returned completely filled out, she was paid three baht. On good days she might bring back twenty completed forms. This meant she would be paid sixty baht, or about two U.S. dollars. Some customers chased her away as soon as they opened the door. Others invited her in and spent the entire time telling Lek about their problems, never filling out a questionnaire.

The new job didn't pay well but it led to something good. During one of her door-to-door calls, a lady told her about her own business, selling cosmetics. She offered Lek a job. With the cosmetic company's catalog and a box of samples, Lek began her second job. With two jobs, Lek was able to afford more supplies for her trips into the jungle. Soon she was able to buy medicine, clothes, and even vegetable seeds. When she visited a jungle village she gave the seeds and clothes to the poor and took care of the ailing elephants at the same time. Her mission was becoming more clear.

Between the jungle and the city there was a terrible secret. Lek discovered it one evening by accident. She had done so well for the French research company, she was asked to head her own team. The company arranged for Lek and her team of four to stay in a Chiang Mai hotel. It was Lek's first time in a hotel. At night she saw three young women in the hotel lobby sitting with their mothers. The youngest girl looked to be about fourteen, and the oldest no more than twenty. Soon a group of men joined them. One of the men seemed to be in charge because he talked the most and the loudest. All of the men asked questions of the girls—very personal questions. Their mothers answered the questions for their daughters. They seemed to be trying very hard to assure the men that their girls should be hired. Lek overheard one mother saying that her daughter was still a virgin. The girls seemed frightened. One of them stared down at the floor, biting her fingernails. The men, Lek concluded, were in a gang. They were buying these girls to use as prostitutes. The mothers were there to sell their daughters.

In the three nights Lek spent at the hotel, she saw a similar meeting take place each night in the lobby, with different girls and mothers. Later she learned that several families of a northern Thai village were part of the ring. It all started when one girl returned home from the city with money, new clothes, and other nice things that villagers normally could not afford. Other village families wanted the same. More mothers traveled to Chiang Mai with their daughters to arrange for work. Lek felt sorry for them, the families and the poor young girls. But she was relieved that she had never heard of this sort of thing happening in Baan Lao or with Khamu people.

When she wasn't trying to sell cosmetics or doing marketing research, and when she wasn't studying and attending classes, Lek carried on her fight to save elephants from abuse. At first, the really mean and abusive mahouts made her so angry she didn't want to help them at all. But with time she decided, mean or not, it was the elephants that mattered, not their cruel masters. To help the animals, she had to go through their mahouts. Besides, the Karen mahouts were among the poorest men she knew. They had literally nothing in the world but their work animals. The logging companies paid them very little. But through this work they could scrape by and keep their families fed. The only way to help all of the elephants, even elephants controlled by mahouts who abused them, was to find a way to educate these mahouts. Lek's efforts worked some of the time. Many mahouts followed her advice. They let Lek use her rucksack of medicine to treat elephants with deep wounds, to cure infections, and to worm the animals. Still, other mahouts continued to live in ignorance. A few mahouts laughed at all of the attention Lek gave to their work animals.

The number of trips away from campus increased. She spent more and more time away from the university. Some of Lek's fellow students began to talk. Seeing her disappear from the university for days at a time made them wonder. Rumors spread. *Lek had a jungle boy lover.* She was missing class to meet her jungle lover. With more trips, the rumors got worse. *She secretly had a baby in the jungle and had to return from time to time to raise it.* When they got back to Lek, she was hurt. But nothing, not even rumors like this, could stop her. Her life had changed. She had found something so important that it began to consume her.

As Lek spent more and more time with the elephants, her studies suffered. One day the academic manager called her in with very bad news. She was not earning enough hours to graduate. Worse, she was spending so much time away that the university's academic committee issued a warning. She was in danger of being suspended from studies. Unless she spent more time in class, she was on the verge of being kicked out. What shame she would bring on the Khamu!

Her advisor suggested that she withdraw from school and return the next year. But one of her professors showed her another way out of the problem. She would withdraw from a couple of courses, and extend her program an additional year. That way she would have more time to attend lectures for the classes she kept, and a way to graduate, even if beyond the normal time for obtaining her degree. That's what she did.

Outside of the university she was doing very well. She was earning all the money she needed to finance her growing elephant rescue mission. She had become a highly successful saleslady. She even supplemented her earnings during special celebrations that turned Chiang Mai into a tourist town. Lek teamed up with her siblings to sell film and souvenirs to the foreigners. More money meant she could do even more to reach the elephants. She could afford to rent a jeep, and that meant she could travel deeper and deeper into the rugged border country. She did not always stop at the border. Sometimes the jeep would stop at the Salawin River, a river that separated Thailand from Burma. Lek would then take a boat across to aid elephants in Burma.

During one of her trips to the border, she met a man she thought to be one of the Christian missionaries. His name was Peter, a man of about thirty. Peter stayed at the same boarding house as Lek. He said he was a volunteer teacher, not a missionary. He taught in a Karen village on the border. The missionaries and boarders all liked Peter. He was cheerful and friendly to all. He told compelling stories about the stark poverty of the village where he taught. Several people at the Christian mission donated old clothes, books, and toys to his cause. Even Lek gave him things because she was so moved by his description of the Karen village.

Deeper and deeper Lek went into the jungle. Deeper and deeper she traveled into Burma. This was not a safe time for such visits. Burma was filled with internal strife. A number of guerrilla organizations existed. An ethnic group called Kachins fought against the military government through its military arm, the Kachin Independence Army. Karen hill tribe people in Burma also opposed the military rulers in the 1980s. Their rebel warriors formed the Karen National Liberation Army. The Karen movement began with a people very much like the Khamu, with mixed animist and Buddhist beliefs. By the time Lek visited the Burmese jungles, the KNLA split into the Christian Karens and the Buddhist Karens. Shan people in Burma formed a rebel army known as the Shan State Army. These various "independence" armies fighting against the government all operated in Burma at the very time when Lek was crossing the border to treat ailing elephants.

It was in 1988 that a major coup took place in Burma, known as the 8888 Uprising. Protestors against the military government suffered severely. On August 8, 1988, the military fired directly into crowds of these protesters. Thousands of deaths followed. The entire country was filled with fear. Lek journeyed to the town of Baan Koh Loh in Burma during this turbulent period. It was a town buried deep in the jungle. The road to Baan Koh Loh disappeared well short of the village. Lek and her elephant rescue team had to abandon their vehicle and travel by foot the rest of the way, a hike that took nearly six hours.

Her driver for the trip, as far as the car could travel, was Lek's Uncle Boon. He once served as a driver in the Thai military. Two years before he began working for Lek, his wife died. He was a changed man after her death. He drank heavily. The only job he could hold was as a porter in the local market, carrying packages for shoppers for a few baht. When Lek began to make regular rescue trips into the jungle, she needed a driver who wasn't afraid to drive on the rugged mountain roads. Uncle Boon volunteered. Despite his drinking, he never touched a drop when he drove for her. That didn't mean he stopped drinking. Once they were safely at their destination, he settled in to a night of drinking. He liked the local corn or rice moonshine. But when the sun came up, he was sober and ready to drive.

As her team arrived in Baan Koh Loh, she saw women, children, and some very old men. But nowhere did she see young men. It seemed very strange. During the night it became even more mysterious as she heard people return to the village. The men had returned. The military government sent soldiers out to the villages to get new recruits. They took almost any able-bodied men they could find. They were snatched up and sent to join the Burmese Army. It wasn't as brutal as what the Japanese had done with their slave labor camps during the war, but it was still a hated practice. Recruits were immediately pressed into combat service, ordered to fight the insurgents. So the villagers of Baan Koh Loh protected their young men by sending them into the bush to hide during the day, returning only at night.

When Lek finished her work in Baan Koh Loh, she asked where the next village was. She was told there was one but no one ever went there. Lek wanted to take her elephant team there and not waste the supplies that had taken so much work to bring into this remote area of Burma. When she asked why no one went there, the villagers told her that outsiders were not allowed. This only made Lek more curious. She packed up her gear and headed for this "unfriendly" village, along with Uncle Boon, two other team members, and a local guide. After several hours hiking up and down the local mountains, they came into what looked like a huge town.

But this village didn't look like a village at all. It was laid out like a logging camp. Instead of seeing only women and children as she did in Baan Koh Loh, there were none of either in the new village. Only men populated this place, men with a surprised look on their faces. They were not just Asian men. She saw a number of foreigners, white men, in the big town. Within twenty minutes of her arrival, a man on horseback rode right up to Lek and ordered her to follow him. He took her to a large hut, apparently the headquarters. Lek had stumbled onto a guerrilla army camp!

When she entered the hut, another surprise awaited her, a pleasant one, or so she thought. Inside was someone she knew. It was Peter the teacher. But he seemed different. He wasn't friendly. There wasn't the usual smile lighting up his face. In fact, he didn't act the same at all. Instead, he began to question her. Why was she here? Who told her to come to this village? Who did she work for? What group? What organization? What government?

Lek was very confused. Peter was not who he said he was. He was a soldier or advisor for the Karen rebel army. He told her to leave and never return. He also said something very odd: *She never saw him there.* He told her as she left that their meeting never took place. She took the hint. When she returned to Chiang Mai she thought about Peter and the all-male "village." It was most likely a training camp for the guerrillas.

After discovering his secret, Lek ran into Peter at the boarding house and at church. But it was the "other Peter," smiling and coaxing others to give him books and clothes for the "poor Karen villagers." In a way this wasn't a lie. The donations did go to poor Karen men, but these men were fighting the government. Peter still acted cheerful around Lek. But since her return, she stayed away from Peter—far away.

The Spirit of Lek Meets the Spirit of Noom: Life, Death, and Beyond!

Lek organized more trips to the borderland. Each time she returned from one of these, a buzz would start among her university friends. As she planned another trip, this time for October, two of her friends asked to go along. To them it was an exciting adventure to journey deep into the Thai-Burmese jungle. Lek agreed to take them and Uncle Boon agreed to drive.

October can be a very strange month weather-wise in Thailand, especially in the mountainous north. Mornings are often bone-chillingly cold, but as the day wears on the temperature can rise to blistering levels. October is also the end of, but still part of, the rainy season. The village that Lek and her little team headed for was hidden deep in the jungle. When the road ended, the small elephant rescue team had to leave their jeep behind and begin what would be a three-day hike to get to the elephants in need. The team spent the first night in a tiny jungle village. They passed other villages on their way. When no village was nearby, they slept in the jungle.

It was a very difficult journey. They may have been the only human flesh that ever passed through this remote Thai-Burmese area, because periodically, swarms of mosquitoes followed them and devoured them. Lek was used to the rough conditions. She had grown up in the jungle. She was taught by one of the greatest shamans that ever lived in that part of Thailand. She knew the plants and trees, and respected the animals that lived there. So hiking through the deep jungle did not bother her at all, at least not until she hit the wall.

Between tropical downpours and attacking mosquitoes, Lek began to weaken as she made her way through the rugged terrain. Her body seemed to be fighting against her desire to stay strong and lead the others to their final destination. She felt weak, then she felt fine, then weak, and on and on. Her head began to ache. But she was the leader of the group. It was a group that picked up two additional members along the way: porters to help carry the large rucksacks through the thick jungle. She had to show the others that she could make it. Slowing down or resting would not be a good signal from their leader. As they approached the village, Lek's headache and fatigue got worse. She also felt a new pain located in her back. Even the veins in her temples seemed to be screaming for relief the pressure was so bad. All she wanted to do when she arrived was to collapse into a long sleep. With a good night's rest she was certain everything would be fine.

When she got to the village she went to the river and plunged her head into the cool waters. She was on fire with fever. The whites of her eyes had turned blood red. The leader of this Karen hill tribe village invited her to stay at his family's house. Lek asked for some aspirin and told him she would sleep a few hours before she began her work. She put her head down thinking she could sleep off her illness. That's when everything changed. That's when the magic began. That's when the door opened. That's when she fell off the mountain. That's when the river swept her down, down its dark and mysterious path into the other world. She was no longer in the jungle. Somehow she was transported to an in-between world. It was a world filled with voices without bodies. She heard Uncle Boon's voice. She heard the voices of her two university friends. It was as if her body lay suspended in space, or stretched out on the bottom of the river, and faint voices reverberated through some bizarre medium, until strange echoes of those voices made it to her ears.

She was no longer burning with fever. She was cold. Her head felt heavy, yet she seemed to be flying all over the place. She spoke to those around her. She did not know what she was saying, but her mouth opened and something came out. What began as a few hours of sleep now became an eternity where time did not matter. That's when they appeared—ghosts, spirits, and memories. Grandfather Noom was there. Her beloved animals, the ones she kept in Baan Lao also came. Her mother appeared.

Lek lost the ability to know where she was. Time was useless. Thinking was insane. Sleep merged with being awake and everything that came into her mind was a messy combination of reality and something else. She couldn't tell if she was half-asleep but waking up, or half-awake and drifting off. At one point Lek found herself on a bamboo bed. Four men were carrying the bed. Later she was tied to the bed. They were taking her away, away from the village she worked so hard to reach. She begged for water. The four men stopped, untied her, and gave her water. Then she saw the others. She saw her cat. She saw her dogs. All of the pets from her childhood danced in front of her. All of the animals that lived in the family compound and the ones that lived in her room, the ones her sister despised so much, they all were there. She entered the door to the other side. As she went back and forth, from hot to cold, tied and untied, they appeared.

The sky was different. It changed from blue to red. Lek felt it change. She felt it move. It was spinning around her. She watched as the cows in Baan Lao appeared. She was no longer on the bamboo bed. She was lying on top of an elephant. It was Chang Thongkam, the golden one. The beloved elephant of her childhood was alive, or if she was dead, Lek was lying atop the ghost of Chang Thongkam. It felt so wonderful to be close to her, to play on her just as she did when all of the children played with her. Soon the trees around Lek began to whirl all about her. Lek fell asleep or passed out.

But her journey into the other world was not finished. She had never left the village at all. Uncle Boon and her two university friends must have carried out her mission because now she was treating the elephants just as she planned. One had a very bad wound. Others had to be wormed. Then things got much worse. There was blood everywhere. Some elephants were missing their eyes. Screaming elephants, elephants in unimaginable pain, penetrated Lek's soul. She wanted to reach out and comfort the bleeding, blind, and screaming animals. She yelled at the mahouts to stop abusing their animals. She tried, but she could not lift her arms. Someone had chained her arms to her bed. What had she done? What horrible thing had led to this?

Somewhere in the blackness, somewhere through the space where she was floating, or through the water where she lay suspended, a familiar voice touched her ears and drifted into her consciousness. It sang a song. It was a happy song. It was the song that meant Lek would drift off into Never-Never Land. It was a song from her early childhood. It was her mother's sweet voice singing the lullaby song she used to sing Lek to sleep. Lek could not see her mother's face, but she wanted to tell her she knew she was there. Lek opened her mouth and something came out—what, Lek did not know.

Her prison was a mattress. Chained or tied, she could not leave it, not even to relieve herself. She felt the wetness of her own urine from time to time. She felt the warmth and horrible smell as she lost control of her bowels. Someone would clean her. Someone would clean her mattress. Then, back to the prison. Someone on the other side was crying. It was her mother. Others were crying. She heard her aunt, Miss Nang. She heard her sister. She tried to talk with Lek. Then she too began to cry. Lek tried to answer them. She tried to pierce the veil and shout words that would reach them on their side. She asked them why they were crying. She asked them what was happening to her. Finally, she told them not to cry. Then all went black into sleep or death. Lek lost consciousness again.

In her dream or perhaps while she was awake someone came to her. She saw him before, just as she crossed over. Now he was standing directly in front of her. It was Grandfather Noom. Behind him was Chang Thongkam. The shaman reached down and extended his arms to the little girl. She grabbed them tightly and he swung her up, up, up to the head of the golden one. Lek was riding on top of her beloved first elephant. Chang Thongkam took her to the river. She put her trunk in the water and then sprayed the dead or sleeping woman with cool river water. When she felt the water on her face, Lek woke up. She tried to reach out and touch her beloved golden friend, but as she did she saw it. She saw a needle stuck deep in her arm. The metal tip was taped to her arm and connected to an intravenous feeding tube that led to a bottle.

Now she was waking up. Now the world around her seemed real. Noom and Chang Thongkam were not there at all. Her mother was there. Lek touched her mother's hand and tried to speak. Nothing came out. She was choking on something that was stuck down her throat, making talking impossible. But as she awoke from the long journey to another world, she saw her mother's face filled with a huge smile, and almost simultaneously, with tears. Phong Sri hugged her daughter and called for the doctor.

Lek had slept for nearly fifteen days. During that time she was in and out of a malarial delirium. Her mother thought Lek would die. She shook so violently with the illness that she had to be tied to her bed. Before she reached the hospital, Uncle Boon tied her to a bamboo bed so they could hike back to the jeep and get her to the hospital. It was and it was not just a dream. Bits and pieces of reality were scattered over fifteen days with hallucinations and physical reactions brought on by malaria.

Lek learned the details of her illness and the crazy thoughts it produced in her from her mother. She told Lek she had many visitors as she fought to recover from the death grip of malaria. Lek could not remember anyone in particular. Everything around her seemed to be filtered through the cloud of the disease. Some reality made its way through the fog of the delirium. She was kept alive with anti-malaria medicine, tracheal feeding tubes, and an intravenous tube that sent much needed fluids and antibiotics into her body. It was the tracheal tube that prevented her from speaking. Just as important as the medical treatment, her mother's words fought off death. Throughout the ordeal Phong Sri told her daughter that she must fight hard. She told Lek that she had to live for her family. She also reminded her of something that another family and another mother might never have thought of. Others needed her. Those others were the elephants she loved so much. Lek must win this battle for them.

Phong Sri helped fill in the void left by fifteen days of being in and out of consciousness. Lek's own crazy recollection of seeing Noom and Chang Thongkam were part of the disease. Her mother said that Lek spoke throughout the two weeks about her elephants. Sometimes her delirious chatter described the way she treated them with medicine. At other times Lek would scream with fear, telling a mahout to stop beating his animal.

As her mother helped her solve her own confusion, Lek began to come out of it. She did not know it at the time, but her mother never left her bedside in the hospital. Phong Sri told her again and again that she must get up. If she stayed in bed and didn't use all of her strength to stand and walk, she would not make it. And if she died, her mother told her, Phong Sri would die too. It was a heart-wrenching daily talk about love and need. Some of it just floated away; some of it got through.

After her fifteen days in that other place, that other world, Lek spent another five days making progress in the hospital. Malaria left its mark on her already small body. Her skin turned yellow. She lost so much weight, that her legs were thin as matchsticks. Much of her hair fell out as a side-effect of the medicine. For weeks, someone had to carry her to the toilet. On one of her trips she saw her reflection in the bathroom mirror. It was frightening. She saw a bony-faced old lady with yellow skin. The first time she tried to walk on her own, her whole body began to shake. She had to stop and vomit.

Slowly, Lek regained enough strength so that she could walk to the hospital exercise room for physical therapy. When her doctors allowed, she returned home to Baan Lao. Her father picked special herbs to help her recover. He boiled these and Lek drank the herbal liquid. Sa-Nguan also made her a special bamboo harness that allowed her to move around despite her weak legs. Phong Sri massaged those legs with herbs every day. Even with all of her time in the hospital and the physical therapy she forced herself to endure for months, Lek had difficulty walking.

Life, Love, and Laundry

Malaria nearly killed her. When she was allowed to leave the hospital, Lek went home—home to Baan Lao, and home to the loving care of her family. But it was not a happy homecoming for her. The simple village of her childhood, where people gathered in the evening to listen to the news on the one transistor radio—that place no longer existed. Her memories of those days were locked away, deep inside her, in a special place. The new face of Baan Lao was nothing like those memories. Bamboo and grass huts were replaced by concrete homes. Khamu customs were being forgotten. Khamu women no longer followed the strict code of their mothers and grandmothers. They now wore shorts around the village when shorts were never allowed in days gone by. Traditional Khamu women did not even show their naked shoulders. More and more women left Baan Lao only to return with men who were not from the area. Some came back smelling of perfume. Some spoke loudly and rudely like the city people Lek encountered on her first trip to the big city. Some told stories of their work as bargirls in the city. Lek did not like the face of change.

It was to this modern version of the tiny jungle village that Lek returned to recuperate from malaria. She was an invalid for nearly three months, trying to regain the strength sapped by the disease. The damage done to her body seemed to be matched by the emotional damage she felt over the change to her village. It wasn't just the people who were different; the jungle itself was changed. The forest that surrounded Baan Lao, which once wrapped it in green beauty, was nearly gone. When Lek woke up each day of her recuperation period, birds no longer greeted her with their beautiful morning song. To hear them now, she had to travel deep into the jungle, something she could not do until she was strong enough to walk.

To make things worse, Lek was a failure. She returned as the first Khamu woman in the entire mountain valley to reach the university—but to do what? She was the one chosen to show others that a hill tribe woman could succeed. After coming so close to success, she was reduced to a helpless young girl whose mother had to care for her. She felt like an injured animal, a tiger once poised to strike now at the mercy of everyone and everything in the jungle. Injured tigers did not live long.

For several weeks after being released from the hospital, Lek dedicated herself to regaining her strength so she could walk without assistance. Recovering from the damage done to her body by the disease was not easy. Little by little, with daily and oftentimes painful exercise, she was able to get back on her feet. Eventually Lek began to walk on her own. One of the first trips she made alone was to Noom's banyan tree. She spoke to his spirit, explaining to Noom how difficult life had become for her. It was after this visit that Lek decided she could not remain in Baan Lao, that she had to make it on her own. She went to her mother to announce her plans. Lek told her that she must leave. She would go back to Chiang Mai and find work. Her mother didn't agree. She didn't think she was strong enough to leave and certainly not strong enough to work. But Lek insisted. She was tired of being a burden on her parents, especially on her mother. There was just one problem. She did not have a single baht to her name to even get to Chiang Mai. Her studies had taken all of her savings. After her bout with malaria, she had nothing left. On the day Lek was to leave the village, her mother surprised her with a gift of love. Phong Sri came to her rescue, giving her daughter six hundred baht, or the equivalent of twenty U.S. dollars to pay for her trip to the city. For her children, Phong Sri was willing to spend her last baht.

Work was not easy after being sick for so long, but Lek was intent on paying her mother back quickly. She tried a number of jobs in Chiang Mai. She became a receptionist for a film company. She worked in a beauty salon. She was a waitress for a short time. Strenuous jobs did not last very long. Still she pushed herself. Even with her limitations she worked long hours, sometimes nearly fifteen hours a day.

The Elephant Lady of Thailand

At the time, Chiang Mai was already a popular tourist town. Nighttime in Chiang Mai was a very busy time. The city's night bazaar is a centuries-old tradition. Tourists take to the streets and spend their money at the bazaar. Little shops and booths line the streets for several city blocks. Vendors sell all varieties of merchandise and food to visitors. Souvenirs are found everywhere, including Thai handicraft, jewelry, silk, and silverware. Lek found a job selling t-shirts in the bazaar. One day the manager of a tour company stopped by and saw Lek in action. He watched her sell shirts to English-speaking tourists. He was impressed with her English and offered her a job as a tour guide. Lek agreed, but continued to work at the night bazaar as well.

Lek was twenty-one when malaria struck. She spent her childhood learning from a wise grandfather and her young adult years learning from university professors. By the time she went to Chiang Mai to earn a living, she had been too busy to do the normal things that young people do. She never dated boys and had never fallen in love. Khamu customs kept her away from boys and dating. The one time it looked as if a young man was interested in her, those customs kept him away from her. While still at the university, a student asked Lek if she would have lunch with him at the school canteen. Lek agreed. She told her would-be lunch date she was Khamu. The next day she watched him keep his distance. He wanted nothing to do with a hill tribe girl.

She promised her parents that she would not lose the traditional ways. She also vowed not to disgrace her family by becoming too familiar with a member of the opposite sex. Some of her university friends wondered about Lek because she clung so strongly to her hill tribe beliefs. To her parents she was the obedient daughter, but to these friends, Lek seemed terribly strange and out of touch with what was going on with young people in Thailand.

Now she was trying to earn a living by working during the day as a tour guide and in the evening selling t-shirts in the night bazaar. One evening a handsome young foreigner came into her shop. He seemed very interested in buying a shirt, but could not agree on the price. Over and over again he tried to bargain with

Lek. After a while, Lek could see that her boss, the shop manager, was getting annoyed with the man. Finally, he bought the shirt and left.

Lek didn't think much about the incident until she saw him again the very next night. He watched her sell the same style shirt to another customer. When he noticed the price was less than he had paid one day earlier, he became angry. He went over to Lek and accused her of cheating him. Lek told him if he bought another shirt she would give him the same discount. He agreed. He also wanted more than a shirt. He liked Lek and kept coming back, night after night to talk to her. To make sure her boss would not get angry, he bought a shirt each time he visited.

He was from Ireland. Lek had met many tourists in her day job, but he was the first Irishman. She did not even know where Ireland was on the map. What she did know was that she liked this handsome foreigner. She liked him a lot. But he couldn't keep buying shirts just to see her. After a while, he would meet her when the t-shirt booth closed and walk her home.

Adam was very honest with Lek. He told her he had a girlfriend back home in Ireland. She told him she did not have a boyfriend. They agreed to be "just friends" and their relationship grew closer. He wasn't like some of the other men Lek met in Chiang Mai, especially the foreigners. They wanted to touch her and get close to her, but Adam respected her customs. At first, she would not even go to dinner with him because she did not believe she should be seen with a man at night. Adam did not push her. He seemed more interested in helping Lek learn more English.

Lek's first official "date" with Adam was not the usual kind. She went to church with him. After this, she agreed to eat dinner with him. He took her to a pizza parlor and she ate pizza for the first time. She didn't like it. Adam saw her more and more. Lek felt something strange was happening to her. But no matter where they went or what they did, Adam never tried to take advantage of her. He respected her beliefs and never touched her. She respected her parents and kept the promise she made to them.

To Lek, Adam was such a different kind of foreigner. He never tried to impress her with money or gifts. In fact, he explained that he had to watch his money and cut costs while he lived in Thailand. Lek was drawn to him more and more. She loved his handsome looks and his frank honesty. Then one day he broke the news. He had to leave. He had to return to his own country. Lek saw him off at the Chiang Mai Airport. It was a difficult goodbye, but she got through it. She understood their friendship had limits. She knew they would not be together forever. Lek knew. She had common sense. She understood. Then she went to her place and it was as if a mountain had fallen on her. All of the reasonable thoughts in her head could not hide from her the one burning truth: she had fallen in love with Adam.

Heartbroken over Adam, Lek decided to bury her sorrow in work. She took a job as the tour operator for a bus company. The company scheduled her to work every day, seven days a week. She continued to write Adam, but now she faced a new crisis, not love, but fatigue from overwork. When she asked her boss to give her time off, he refused, telling her the company could not afford to hire someone to cover the days she did not work. That's when Lek decided to make a change. Still stinging from her first love, and faced with endless hours of work, she decided to start her own business.

Her landlord agreed to let her rent space in her building for seven thousand baht a month, roughly equal to two hundred and thirty-three dollars, U.S. Starting her new business was easy. She simply hung out a sign: *Wash, Dry, and Iron Service*. Without a washing machine or a dryer, Lek began her business. She offered such cheap prices that she was soon overwhelmed with work. Her washing machine consisted of a large washbowl and a brush. Her dryer was the rooftop and sun. She would take a load of wet, hand-washed clothes to the roof and squeeze the water out by hand and let the sun do the rest. When the clothes were dry she would iron them.

Lek's customers were extremely pleased with her work. For a very small price they had clean, well-pressed clothes, and thanks to Lek's sense of pride, their clothes were always returned on time. This just brought more business Lek's way. In fact, it was more than she could handle. She had to enlist the help of her family. Soon she was joined by three of her younger sisters, Phan Nee, Sakorn, and Petrin. The four sisters ran Lek's laundry business. Customers included men from the U.S. military stationed in Thailand for temporary duty. The sisters laundered their clothes including their underwear. This caused a serious problem with the hill tribe laundry team.

Khamu hill tribe people believe that a person's underwear is a forbidden object to touch. Just to walk beneath the underwear hanging on a clothesline will insult the spirits. So does walking beneath a female skirt hanging to dry. It's a very conservative system of beliefs, but for Lek's little sisters, it was something they dare not violate. That left just Lek to wash the underwear! There was too much. It was impossible for just one person to finish it all on time. Lek got an idea. She bought scratch-off lottery tickets for her sisters. If they won, they could buy a washer and dryer and her problem would be solved. If they lost, and they surely would, they would want to try again, and again, and again! But the only way they could afford to buy the tickets was by helping her get the laundry back to customers on time. That meant they had to help her with the lowly underwear, which they eventually did. Somehow luck was with the sisters and they won enough from the lottery tickets to buy the washer and dryer.

Lek's first experience running her own business was a good one. She learned a lot about pleasing customers. She also enjoyed this time with her sisters. They ran the business so efficiently, washing everything by hand, that they were able to afford a washing machine. That made life much easier for all of them. Every fifteen days Lek would have a payday. Each sister received her hard-earned share of the profits. As good a businesswoman as she proved to be, something beckoned her. Something out there called to her. Something like the spirits Noom taught her were a part of her, of the Khamu, and of the jungle. Lek had to find a way to answer. She had to find a way back to her beloved elephants.

Death Trap

When Lek was fully recovered from malaria she planned another trip into the jungle. During her recuperation period, Uncle Boon, her trusty driver, went back to being a porter in the market. He was pleased to hear about a new trip and very happy to leave his job to once again drive for Lek's team. Lek told him they would be traveling into Burma, into the mysterious area known as the Karen State. This was some of the most rugged country imaginable. She told Uncle Boon to find a four-wheel drive truck.

The Karen State is a region in Myanmar bordering the northwestern part of Thailand. The Thai provinces of Tak and Mae Hong Song share borders with this mountainous part of Myanmar. For many years the entire area has been home to various insurgency groups with the most prominent one being the Karen National Liberation Army. It was not just the rugged terrain that challenged Lek's elephant team. Danger lurked in the form of armed men who did not welcome strangers into their secret campsites.

This trip would be very different. It was not really a rescue mission. Even though she packed her normal medicine and supplies, Lek was after something that she had only heard about. She wanted to see how the local tribesmen captured wild elephants. As someone devoted to helping these animals, she had to see how they came into captivity in the first place. The only way to do this was to go on a wild elephant roundup.

Elephants, as the long-time beasts of burden in Asian countries, have been used primarily in the logging industry. Raising them in captivity is not practical. First, the mother carries her baby elephant through a pregnancy that lasts nearly two years. Once born, babies stay with their mothers and nurse for up to two more years. During this time they are essentially useless as worker elephants. So instead of taking the long time and enormous effort to raise elephants, the Karen hill tribe people capture wild elephants and train them to work. Lek was on her way to the Karen State to see how the capture took place.

She knew it would be a difficult trip. Their first obstacle was the border crossing from Thailand into Burma. The Thai military guards were suspicious from the start. Lek told them she was going to the Karen State, the hotbed of anti-government rebel groups. The border guards spent several hours searching every container of Lek's supplies. When they saw all of the medical supplies which Lek always packed for rescue missions, they suspected that Lek was engaged in illegal activity in the Karen State.

The guards were very rough on Lek and her party. They conducted a search of the truck that began in the morning and did not finish until early evening. By the time the search was over, the border post was closed. This meant Lek had to scramble for a place to spend the night. She and her team made it to a nearby village where they found lodging at the local temple.

The next day they entered the Karen State. In a very short time it became clear that the truck was useless. The jungle was too thick. The only way to get to the area where wild elephants were sighted was by foot. They abandoned the truck at a village and added six Karen porters to help carry the supplies. Even though the hike was difficult, it was through some of the most beautiful country imaginable. The team followed a mountain ridge. To look down was to see a grand vista of several more mountains. They were so high up on the ridge that mountaintops appeared below them. From time to time they found themselves walking through a thick mountain mist. It was like walking through a cloud. The wind, altitude, and thick wet blanket of mist combined to chill Lek and the others. By nightfall they reached their destination, a village well inside the Karen State. This was where the poachers were. Lek told them that she was conducting a "research project" about wild elephants. That's all she had to say. No one was interested in asking her any other questions. She was accepted. The only thing she had to do was to wait until the Karen elephant trappers were ready.

The Karen preparation for the hunt was a ritual unto itself. First, they could not leave for the trap area until they felt it was a lucky day. When Lek arrived, it was not a good day. She would have to wait until the Karen men decided it was time. A trapper's honesty was also put to the test. No known liars were allowed on the team. A couple of rules had to be obeyed for several days before departing. Seven days prior to the hunt, no physical contact with a woman was permitted. For the same period, no man could look in a mirror. Walking beneath clothes hung out to dry was banned. As strange as these rules were, the Karen believed that disobeying any one of them risked death, immediately or during the actual capture.

Building a trap that holds stampeding elephants takes months, but to the Karen it is well worth it despite the danger. Neither injury nor death can change their minds. Lek learned of one Karen man whose father was killed during an elephant roundup. A few more of his relatives met the same fate. This did not stop him from taking part in trapping elephants. Capturing even a few elephants guaranteed a nice little income for him and this meant food for his family.

The trap was built into the ground so that the elephants were led into a tunnel from which they could not escape. The walls of the tunnel were made of long logs stacked on top of each other, nearly twenty feet high. At its widest point the tunnel trap measured nearly two hundred meters or about six hundred feet across. From the wide opening at the start of the tunnel, the tunnel chute extended some four hundred and fifty feet. Once the elephants entered the trap, a large gate made turning around and escaping next to impossible. The gate was constructed of logs bound together forming a solid wall. The ends of the logs were carved to fine sharpened points. The entire gate was then lifted high above the ground, leaving the pathway to the trap open to the stampeding elephants. A strong rope held the gate in place. When the last elephant was past the gate, securely inside the trap, a man cut the rope and down slammed the gate, spearing the ground with the sharp ends, and preventing any elephants from escaping.

Even though Lek was in the village of the elephant trappers, she was still a two-day hike from the trap itself. She prepared enough food for a week. She also hired a Karen porter to stay close to her. She was warned that entering the realm of wild elephants was extremely dangerous. She needed someone with local knowledge to help her survive. Lek, Uncle Boon, and their Karen porters joined ten Karen trappers. Once the "lucky" day arrived, they began their trek to the trap area.

On the way, Lek thought about her trip long ago to Ghost Creek. This trip, like that one, went through pristine and beautiful land. The jungle forest was thick. They passed natural wonders like giant bamboo that seemed to tower over everything like giant redwood trees. But for all of the beauty she experienced along the way, she could not get one thought out of her mind: They were going to make slaves of these magnificent animals!

As they got closer to the territory where wild elephants roamed, Lek's Karen porter warned her. They were about to enter an incredibly dangerous place. One wrong move meant death. The elephants here were nothing like the elephants she was used to, the ones she nursed back to health. She helped heal trained elephants. They rarely posed a threat. They were like her beloved Chang Thongkam. Not now. Things were very different now. She was about to encounter wild elephants. She was trespassing through the territory of gargantuan creatures that ruled the jungle. Wild elephants were in command. Their sense of territoriality meant they would fight to the death to protect this land. Their sense of family meant they would protect their own. Females with calves were particularly dangerous. Males seeking females were just as dangerous if not more aggressive. Any threat to their habits and habitat provoked incredibly fast charges aimed directly at the threat. A human making any noise at all was just such a threat. Lek was such a threat.

It wasn't long after entering elephant territory that confusion broke out. Lek heard something but didn't know exactly what it was, just that it seemed to scare everyone in her party. It sounded like a thunderous CLAP or BANG! As soon as she heard it, her Karen porter and the Karen poachers all disappeared up trees. Wild elephants were coming. Someone yelled from a tree that they were close. Lek ran for the nearest tree. Luckily her years spent in the jungle taught her how to climb quickly. She climbed as high as she could. She saw Uncle Boon scrambling down below her. He picked the wrong tree, climbing over a nest of bees. She watched him running on the jungle floor trying to escape the approaching stampede while fending off attacking and angry bees. It would have been a funny scene except that danger was fast approaching.

Then Lek saw them. A large group of elephants passed below her, slowed now to a walk. Lek did not move at all as they went by. She could barely allow herself to breathe. She was trying so hard not to make any noise or movement that would tell the elephants that humans had entered their domain. Her heart was pounding. She watched in amazement. They were walking so freely. They looked, well, to Lek they looked absolutely elegant. They really did seem to own the jungle, at least this tiny part of it. They showed their confidence with free and easy movement. This was where they could walk and run and play. Nothing was quite as beautiful as watching animals so incredibly free.

Two babies were in this passing group. As she watched them, that terrible thought that invaded her mind earlier returned. She knew something that the elephants did not. Perched high up in a tree, admiring the freedom of the animals she loved the most in the entire world, she held a secret. This family of elephants, the elegant, free-strutting group below her, the one protecting two babies, this group might soon be made slaves to the poachers. Her first instinct was to leave and never come back but she could not. She was stuck in this tree and had voluntarily joined the Karen trappers. She couldn't leave.

Once the elephants passed by, the Karen poachers and Lek got down and headed to a shallow river stream not far away. The Karen instructed Lek that to avoid being detected by the elephants, they must walk in the middle of this stream. Lek did as she was told. When the river grew muddy this meant elephants were just ahead, bathing or crossing the stream, roiling up the mud and silt until it reached her. Each time this happened, the Karen men would look for trees in case they had to make a mad escape from charging elephants.

The river water was warm, making the soggy trek much easier. After two hours of river walking the Karen decided it was safe to walk on the land again. As Lek left the river for dry land, Uncle Boon saw something disturbing. Blood was running down Lek's legs. She lifted her shirt and discovered several leeches sucking away, drinking her blood. With Uncle Boon's help and with the aid of a lit cigarette, Lek was able to remove them all. Most of the river walkers had their own leeches to remove, but Lek seemed to have the most popular blood, attracting more leeches than anyone else.

It was at the very end of this long day, a day filled with hiking, tree climbing, river walking, and bloodletting that they reached the trap. The sun was setting. The Karen poachers had built small huts high up in the trees overlooking the trap. These would be the homes for everyone involved in the roundup. One large tree in particular had a clear view of where the trap ended. The hut built for this tree had the perfect view, allowing its occupants to actually see inside the trap. Lek was in this hut. Once she entered, she could not go down until the wild elephants were trapped and the danger had completely passed. Eating, sleeping, and toilet breaks all had to be done in the hut. There could be no turning back now. Any noise down below would scare the elephants away from the area. Some of the party were cigarette smokers, but smoking was strictly forbidden high up in the trees. The Karen told her that elephants were especially sensitive to smoke.

Lek and Uncle Boon shared the same tree hut for the night. The next morning the trees seemed to be deserted except for the two of them. The Karen men had left without a sound. Down below were two men standing by the huge gate of the trap. It would be their job to slam the gate shut once the elephants entered the trap. Hours passed until Lek heard the same kind of BANG she heard before. This was followed by the sounds of the jungle being crushed by running elephants. Tree branches snapped. Bushes were flattened. The sounds grew louder and Lek knew they were coming toward the trap. Now she began to "feel" the onrushing elephants. The ground beneath her tree began to shake. The entire tree was vibrating and swaying with her in it.

Lek saw them. She looked into their eyes and saw the look of sheer terror in these proud and elegant beasts. They were running straight for the trap. Behind them Karen poachers threw firecrackers to scare them into running toward the trap. Lek was shocked at the chaos below her tree hut. To her, it was more than chaos; it was sheer madness! The older elephants in the stampeding herd seemed to be crying out in painful shrieks of anger. The babies screamed with the fear of a child being beaten mercilessly for no reason. Lek was growing sick to her stomach. She made a mistake. She had made a very serious mistake in allowing herself to be a part of this. Now she was frozen in place. Her mind could not handle the sights and sounds below. Her heart was shattered with the raw emotion of the moment.

She closed her eyes and wrapped her arms around the tree trunk. She was holding on physically, but losing it mentally.

The screaming seemed to go on for hours. When the gate finally closed, five elephants were captured for life, ripped from their jungle kingdom, and sentenced to a lifetime of labor for their human captors. Lek watched them struggle defiantly inside the trap. One bull elephant rammed the log walls of the trap, trying unsuccessfully to break out. The group became so frustrated that they began to fight each other. Every pair of elephant eyes had the unmistakable look of panic. It was no use. Their life as free and wild elephants was over. Lek began to get dizzy. Her throat was dry and breathing itself was difficult. As she watched the struggle below, every part of her body began to tremble. She saw blood coming from one of the smaller elephants. The scene was so appalling that she wet herself. Her eyes filled with tears and nothing could stop her from crying.

The Karen poachers successfully trapped the elephants. By the time the gate slammed shut, it was nightfall. Lek was also trapped, way up in her tree hut for the night. She could not leave. It was too dangerous. Other elephants could attack. She was forced to listen all night to the cries of the defeated elephants. She asked Uncle Boon to tie her to the tree. Every ounce of energy was spent crying and shaking. Without help, she would roll out of the hut to her death. But her nightmare had only begun. All night long she heard the elephants struggling below. There could be no sleep. This was the way of the jungle spirit telling her that something horrible had taken place. It would be her punishment. She had to listen to their painful moans. It was as if Grandfather Noom bound her to the tree and forced her to face the agony that comes when something totally free in nature is stripped of that freedom.

Lek remained there all night in a state of utter confusion. She wrestled with strange mental emotions. She suffered physical pain, trembling, dizziness, and breathing problems. From time to time she would look down through the black jungle night. Her eyes would adjust to the darkness until they could make out large round gray masses. They were masses in motion, seemingly in constant motion, although very slow motion. These were the captured ones. They were now spent from their all-day battle to stay free. She heard them speak, elephants speaking to other elephants. In very low voices, the beaten down animals said something to one another. What—Lek had no idea. To her they seemed to be comforting each other, cooing, echoing tender notes of care.

When the sun came up the next day she understood why. They were indeed talking. Four of them continued to chatter, moving slowly around a fifth one, the one lying on the ground. From time to time, one of four circling elephants would kick the fifth one, the prone one. She was dead. The roundup had killed her. When Lek realized what happened, she began to throw up. She wanted out. She wanted to go home. She wanted to leave this awful place and never come back. But for two more days, Lek had to remain. The Karen told her that when wild elephants are captured, other wild elephants will seek revenge, so no one could leave until enough time passed. For two more days, Lek had to endure the view from above of what had become a death trap.

Death trap: The walls of the tunnel were made of long logs stacked on top of each other, nearly twenty feet high. At its widest point the tunnel trap measured nearly two hundred meters or six hundred feet across.

The Elephant Lady of Thailand

The hut built for this tree had the perfect view, allowing its occupants to actually see inside the trap. Lek was in this hut. Once she entered, she could not go down until the wild elephants were trapped and the danger had completely passed.

Lek standing at the end of the death trap.

Phaajaan: Part I - The Ritual to Destroy Love

Lek saw the beginning of the end of freedom for her beloved elephants when she watched them herded into the trap. It was a horrible sight. She would force herself to go to other roundups. What she saw there made her physically ill. It left deep mental scars. But she knew she was one of the few people who could help the trapped animals with her skills and medicine. On one trip she photographed traps so others would see what she saw, and perhaps, feel the same tormenting pain she felt. During another visit she watched as the trap door slammed down with great force but the gatekeeper cut the rope too soon. The sharp spears of the door's bottom fell on the back of the last elephant entering the trap. The once great king of a wild elephant died an unspeakably painful death.

But as terrible as the elephant trap was, when it did not kill the elephant in the process this was only the beginning of the animal's agony. There was something even worse than the traps. There was and still is a practice that can only be described as ripping the heart out of an elephant. That practice has a special name, a name from a dialect of northern Thailand. It is known as phaajaan, pronounced FAH-JAHN. Lek's experience with phaajaan would be life-changing. It would be the thing that would see her mission in life become crystal clear. It would inspire her to start her own company to save the tortured animals. It would move her to seek an end to the practice. In her quest to do both, it was her own life that was nearly ended.

Roughly translated, phaajaan means to separate or divide. In a very real sense it means to destroy the love or bond between two living beings. While elephants are the only animals to go through the phaajaan, it is also practiced on humans. Village shamans, shamans just like Grandfather Noom, practice phaajaan when called upon. Instead of divorce, or instead of allowing star-crossed lovers to continue to love each other, parents ask the shaman to separate the pair using phaajaan. A family must have a good reason, one that satisfies the shaman. The shaman will refuse to perform phaajaan unless he deems the reason worthy. Once accepted, the family must pay a "spirit tax" ranging from two hundred baht to over five hundred baht.

The Elephant Lady of Thailand

The shaman guides the family through the ceremony. Each step is intended to break the bond of love. Where two lovers are insane with love, phaajaan is designed to beat back the excitement and replace it with boredom. The first step is to find broken objects. The family is ordered to collect common but broken household items, seven to be exact. Broken cups, glasses, or mirrors—it really does not matter what, as long as they are found in the family and therefore represent the unity of the family. These seven broken objects are buried in a place that itself symbolizes destruction. If possible, they are buried in the grave of a criminal. The grave of a murderer is considered the best burial place. At the gravesite, candles and joss sticks of incense are lit. The shaman then casts various spells that break the bond between the two. According to the folklore of hill tribe people, the once passionate lovers lose their desire for each other within days or weeks.

Phaajaan is also used with elephants. It is used to break one of the strongest bonds in nature, the love between a baby elephant and its mother. It can be used to separate a domestic elephant from the herd it considers its family, or to break a wild elephant just as a wild horse is broken. But the ritual for any of these animals—domestic or wild, babies or adults—is a thousand times more painful and a million times crueler than the one used for humans. Phaajaan for elephants involves unbelievable brutality and a torture chamber with the frighteningly descriptive name of the "crush."

When phaajaan is performed to separate a baby or calf elephant from its mother, the baby is normally from one to three years old. A calf elephant is one of the most beautiful creatures on earth. In the first several months of life, it depends largely on its mother for survival, so in addition to its tender beauty, it is all but helpless without its mother. The love between mother and calf is incredibly strong. The ritual to break this bond and destroy this love begins without pain. Village elders write seven names on seven separate scraps of paper. The names are revered for their power to bring good fortune. Each piece of paper is hidden inside one of seven bunches of bananas. The elephant calf is led to the seven bunches until it devours one. The remaining six are checked and the missing name, which is the one buried in the bunch eaten, is the name given to the elephant for good luck. It is good luck in the eyes of the villagers that a successful phaajaan will occur. It is bad luck for the poor calf that must go through the ritual.

Next, just as in the human version, special ingredients are required for the phaajaan to work. An array of edible and nonedible objects is readied. Two live chickens are required. Tradition demands that they must be the same color. Add to these four candles, three incense sticks, fresh cut flowers—of any color other than red—and two bottles of rice whiskey.

Village women are required to do all of the cooking that the ceremony demands. Two kinds of rice are prepared. The first is glutinous rice, a staple food in northern Thailand, also called sticky rice because, once cooked, it sticks together. It is rolled up into little balls and eaten with fish or meat. In addition to the sticky rice, a small bowl of unmilled rice, or rice in its natural state, is present. The women also prepare a special potion, mixing holy water with turmeric, a yellowish spice known for ages as having both medicinal and spiritual properties.

The preparation that comes before the crush is extremely detailed. The presiding shaman will ensure nothing is missing. The ritual requires a specialist among shamans, one known as an elephant shaman. This means he is well experienced in phaajaan and has years of knowledge about the habits and even the psychology of elephants. This knowledge plus the shaman's own in-depth understanding of spells, spirits, nature and even magic, all must be brought to bear.

The number seven is considered special, so certain items come in sevens, such as the seven broken household items when phaajaan is practiced on people. Seven foods are chosen from among those typically eaten by elephants. These usually include bananas, pineapples, and watermelon. Elephants also enjoy tamarind fruit, which tastes both sweet and sour, as well as sugar cane, papaya, and coconut. Seven local plant stems are also set out. These are used to stir a special mixture that is said to cast a spell over the animal. The stems must contain thorns to be effective.

The terror to come does not come from these ingredients, but from the equipment used to subdue the baby elephant as well as its mother. Hobble chains or hobble ropes are readied. These will be fitted snugly around the front and rear legs of the elephant to keep it from running or making any kind of fast movement as it is dragged kicking, screaming, and crying to the crush. Rope used during phaajaan is made from the bark of a local tree. There are a number of objects available to inflict great pain upon the mother and her baby. Some are crude hand spears with wooden handles and sharp metal points, bent in half to allow the holder to hack through the tough elephant skin from above. Hand clubs are used to beat the animals into submission. Long elephant spears are needed to jab the elephants from a safe distance to keep them walking in the right direction, toward a tree or toward the torture chamber itself. But by far the primary piece of equipment for the phaajaan is the torture chamber known as the crush.

Phaajaan: Part II – The Tears of an Elephant

Bringing a baby elephant to the crush is one of the most heart-wrenching scenes imaginable. There is a look that will burn deeply into the consciousness of anyone looking on, of anyone who views any video record of phaajaan, of almost anyone in the world except those who take part in the practice, or those who pay to have an elephant trained by this method. The look is two-fold. It is the shocked face of the baby elephant being led to the crush; and it is the frightened face of the mother watching her infant being led to the crush. For both it's really one common face; it is the look of utter horror. Both have bulging eyes that speak of total fear and sadness.

Elephants are born with large brains. Their ability to communicate with each other is well documented. They use a system of vocal sounds, tactile signals, and smell. With such a complex system they know how to maintain family bonds, warn of danger, and compete for mates. When phaajaan is used to break the bond between mother and baby, fear and sadness take over. Everything about their facial expressions communicates the unmistakable conclusion that these animals feel real emotions. If the shrieks aren't convincing, then the bulging eyes and flood of tears are.

There also must be bewilderment and confusion inside of the elephants, inside their brains, their minds, wherever the elephant psyche or soul resides. Why, after twenty-two months of carrying this baby inside her, is the mother now witnessing the torture of that baby? Why, after suckling with its mother, does the baby now see its mother chained to a tree while up to fifteen two-legged animals poke the baby with knives and spears, and beat it so mercilessly? What happened to nature? How did life change so shockingly fast to see two elephant hearts crushed to death? Giant tears fall in a deluge down the rough-skinned face of both mother and child. There may not be any more searing look in all of the animal kingdom. The elephants take on the tearful gaze of a human creature at the precise moment when several humans become savage animals.

Those who believe in phaajaan also believe that it cannot be performed near the home of the elephant owner or near the mahout who will inherit the trained elephant. The reasons for this are simple yet somewhat incredulous. An elephant shaman must remain in control of the phaajaan. It is believed that an owner may try to stop the procedure once he sees how cruel it is. The other reason involves revenge. Hill tribe people who practice the ritual strongly believe that if a baby elephant is released from the crush too early, it will seek revenge, attacking its mahout, its owner, or their relatives.

Phaajaan can vary in the details. How it is performed may be different at villages in northern Thailand or in Burma. Lek did not focus on the differences, only on the ritual's constant infliction of pain. The typical scene is one of a hot, dusty village where everyone seems to be excited about the ritual. Men and young boys generally take part as either active jabbers, sticking sharp hand spears or long elephant spears into the thick skin of the elephants. Everyone seems to be smiling. As sad as the event is for the animals, phaajaan is a special occasion for the people, something out of the ordinary, so whether they are jabbers or just watchers, everyone is having a good time.

It begins by dragging the mother to a tree. The separation process requires forcing the mother to witness her baby being broken. Therefore, the tree is located near the crush itself. The mother is hobbled with ropes or chains, and can only walk

The Elephant Lady of Thailand

haltingly where the villagers force her to walk like a prisoner with chained hands and feet for a court appearance. She is literally trussed up with thick ropes so that men on each side can pull her, controlling her every movement. Other men with long elephant spears cut her with their jabs, making corrections in her direction with sharp strikes to her sides. While it is true that elephants have very thick skin, one inch thick in places, there is nothing to stop the pain when sharp metal spears penetrate that skin. Throughout the phaajaan dozens upon dozens of cuts are inflicted on the animals. The two most sensitive areas for any elephant are around the mouth and the ears. The men taking part in the phaajaan do not spare either place from their blows. In fact, it is part of the procedure to spear the elephant's ears as punishment or reinforcement. Large splotches of blood from open cuts are typical during the phaajaan. Pulled by ropes that cut her skin, the mother elephant hobbles, nearly seven thousand pounds forced along a dusty path to a tree or to a cluster of trees.

Once the men have her where they want, they bind her so tightly to the tree that this mammoth animal looks as if she is suspended, its neck noosed up high and tight to the tree with one series of ropes, and its rear fastened to the same tree or to a nearby tree. The huge elephant can barely move a muscle and her eyes are trained on the cage twenty or thirty feet away. That cage is the crush where the baby is taken.

Village men and boys drag the small calf to the crush. Like her mother, the baby is all bound up with ropes. One man pulls a rope that controls her front legs, and another pulls one that controls her rear legs. It is much easier to pull the baby up to the crush since she's several thousand pounds lighter. Despite this, one man strikes the calf without mercy with his long spear. Another man stands back, away from the pullers and jabbers, giving directions to everyone. Rope burns covering the baby elephant's body tell the story of her struggle to remain free. Once at the front opening of the crush, her fight is nearly gone. Even if it wasn't, she is about to enter a torture cell that will break her spirit and destroy the natural love between mother and child.

The crush looks like a small pen, a rectangular structure approximately seven feet high by seven feet long. It is just wide enough to force a baby elephant inside. The sides are nothing more than double logs, one set three feet above the ground, and a second set three feet higher. The double logs fit into holes carved into four strong corner posts. Once securely into the crush chamber, the baby cannot move without hitting the sides of the cage. If she lets her trunk fall outside of the crush in a futile effort to stretch or breathe freely, a man with a club pounds on her trunk until she brings it back inside. Another man sits on top of the crush with a hand spear, periodically pounding her head, stabbing it with the spear's head, and teaching her to forget everything she learned in her brief time on the planet. The ropes binding the calf are arranged so that any sudden lurch or thrust by the baby will cause the ropes to tighten around it even more, causing deep rope burns.

The elephant shaman begins the separation ritual. His first order of business is to cast a spell that will destroy the mother's love for her calf. He issues the spell over two food items, the sticky rice and bananas. Once cast, mother and baby are fed the special food. The screaming mother is taken away. The ropes that bound her so tightly to the tree are removed and she is led away, far out of sight of her calf. The ritual continues, turning darker.

The villagers taking part in phaajaan place a spirit house next to the crush. This is a small wooden shelter that the shaman will use to conduct the rest of the ceremony. All of the assembled ingredients are now in the spirit house, ready to be used by the shaman. The shaman takes a sharp knife and slits the throat of one of the two chickens. This causes the chicken, mortally wounded and bleeding uncontrollably, to run chaotically around the area. From this the calf is to see that life and love have their limits. The second chicken is hung by its neck on the spirit house itself. Eventually both chickens die— one bleeding to death and the other by hanging. They are then plucked and gutted. Both are scalded in boiling water and set out with the other ingredients as offerings to the spirits who control the ceremony.

The shaman takes one of the chickens and cuts the head off. He does this so that he can read the bones of the chicken. Different hill tribe people have different ways of reading bones. One, for example, looks to see the shape of the beak after it is cut completely out of the head. A long and straight beak means the calf will live long. It also means that it will grow up loving its owner. This is the best possible omen for the owner. A crooked beak means just the opposite. The calf will be lazy and sickly. Its owner will have the worst luck with an elephant cursed with this sign.

Special chanting begins. The shaman chants for the better part of an hour over burning incense. As he does, he stirs the mixture of turmeric and holy water with the seven thorny stems. Once the holy water is ready, the shaman sprinkles it over the head of the calf. As he does, he has with him a special instrument, an elephant hook possessed of special magical properties.

The shaman mounts the baby just as a rider gets on a horse. He is the first human being to sit atop the elephant and this terrifies the calf. With the magic hook the shaman strikes the calf three times, symbolizing its submission to human training and teaching. Now it is ready. Now it will receive one of two treatments. When it does not resist, it will be fed a small amount of food. When it does resist, it will be hit, whipped, clubbed, or speared. Before it understands the difference, the calf will be tortured over and over again. Before it realizes that no movement means no pain, it will twist and turn and the ropes that bind it will cut the baby's skin again and again.

The shaman only starts the process of training. Once he shows the calf what causes pain and what leads to food, he turns the training over to a mahout. It is not just any mahout, but one selected specially by the shaman as an expert who can lead the young elephant to the right path. There will be brutal lessons for a number of days, up to seven. Some calves stop fighting a few days before this. Some die in training. But the mahout will beat and cut the calf over and over again until it stops resisting. Once the mahout takes over, the shaman tends to the wounds caused by the cuts and the ropes burns. One beats the baby elephant without mercy and the other tries to keep the animal alive. It is a devastatingly tragic cycle for the baby.

The contract between the shaman and the owner states that once phaajaan is complete, the elephant must be ready to work. This is closer to a guarantee than an educated guess. This is why very experienced elephant shamans are used and equally experienced mahouts finish the training in the crush. Nothing can be left to chance. Either the elephant will do what the shaman has promised under the contract, or there will be no payment. Phaajaan is not a free service. Several thousand baht equivalent to several hundred U.S. dollars are charged for phaajaan. A male elephant is considered harder to "break" than a female, so the fee is higher.

It is estimated that only half of all elephants subjected to phaajaan become useful workers, either as laborers in logging camps or as entertainment for tourists. The rest either die or go insane from the extreme cruelty of the crush. The emotional shock of a forced separation from its mother on a young elephant's nervous system is so great that there have been reported cases of elephants trying to commit suicide rather than continue their training. Some try to crush their own skulls by striking their heads against one of the four thick wooden posts of the crush. Elephants that die in the crush often die of a broken heart, somehow sensing that they will never again be rejoined with their mothers. For every worker elephant, Lek could only see the tears that led to domestication. For every elephant show of any kind performed for tourists, she knew that behind the various tricks the tourist elephants performed, the animals suffered incredible pain from their torture. Nothing in her life seemed to affect Lek as much as the phaajaan. But what could she do?

The Elephant Lady of Thailand

The crush looks like a small pen, a rectangular structure approximately seven feet high by seven feet long. It is just wide enough to force a baby elephant inside.

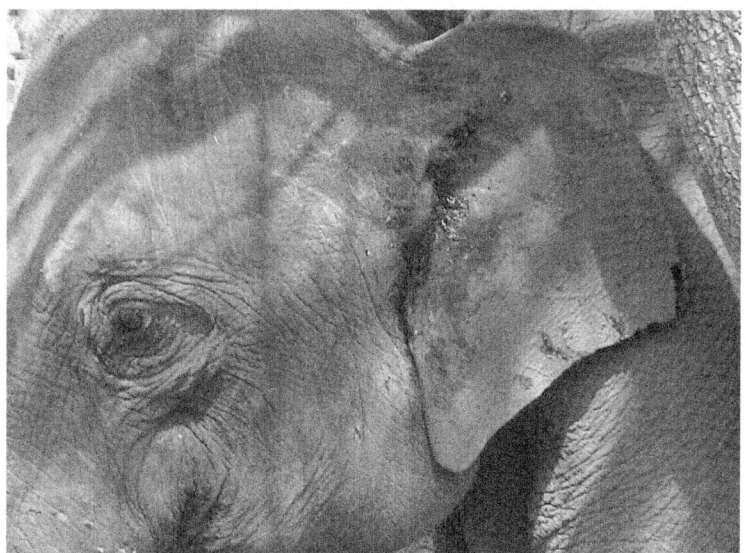

There will be brutal lessons for a number of days, up to seven. Some calves stop fighting a few days before this. Some die in training. But the mahout will beat and cut the calf over and over again until it stops resisting.

Dennis W. Shepherd

Flames That Would Not Die

Lek and her sisters earned a living running their laundry business in Chiang Mai. But just making money did not satisfy Lek's needs. Her heart was split between the elephants that needed her, and the Irishman she found and lost all too quickly. She had only known Adam for six months, but it was long enough to fall in love with him. The two continued to write each other. Lek kept him informed about the things going on in her life, especially her entry into the world of business. Then, one day Lek got a letter from Adam that would drastically change her future. He had been away for a little over two years, working hard to save money. He was saving so he could return. Adam asked her if she wanted a business partner. He was willing to come back and make Thailand his home—permanently!

Upon returning to Thailand, Adam wanted more than to be business partners. He asked Lek to marry him. Lek loved him and he loved Lek, but still a great mountain stood between them: her family. Marrying outside of the Khamu hill tribe was bad enough, but marrying a complete foreigner was the worst thing a Khamu girl could do. During the short time Lek and Adam had spent together, he had never visited her village. Now he insisted that she take him to Baan Lao. Lek was afraid. She knew the Khamu customs and taking a foreigner to meet her family would just raise questions and even—fear!

The two lovers decided that the only way out of their dilemma was to visit Lek's village. When they arrived, it was as if Adam was the only animal in the zoo. Everyone in Baan Lao came out to see him. They stared. They laughed. They turned to each other in little groups and whispered to each other about the stranger from a strange land, from a country called Ireland. The older villagers were fascinated with Adam's looks, especially his blue-green eyes.

Lek worried that Adam would have trouble dealing with the harsh conditions. There were very few creature comforts like air-conditioning or running water. The toilets were of the Thai squat-down variety. But Adam was strong. He made himself at home almost instantly and never complained. It was Lek who had the biggest problem in the village, and the problem was her mother.

Leaving Adam with a group of villagers, Phong Sri pulled her daughter into a room for a private discussion. Immediately she wanted to know one thing: had Lek allowed the foreigner to touch her? Khamu women are carefully protected from outside influences and even skin-to-skin touching is taboo. When Lek confessed to holding hands with Adam, this alone sent her mother reeling. In her mind, even minor contact meant that Lek was no longer pure. The only way to cure the insult, an insult directed at the spirits worshipped by the Khamu, was by marriage. So upset was Phong Sri that she went to her ancestor spirit house to pray for forgiveness.

When Lek told Adam about this, he offered to help by asking her parents for her hand in marriage. By marrying Lek, he would relieve her mother of the insult, the spirits would be appeased, and two lovers could enter a new phase in their young lives as husband and wife. Adam had to present his offer of marriage to Lek's family. Since her parents did not speak English, Lek translated for him as he spoke the words. It was very awkward, but it worked. Adam was given permission to marry Phong Sri's daughter upon payment of the ghost fee, a small fee intended as an offering to the spirits that guarded the community. At the time this amounted to not much more than one U.S. dollar. Some Khamu parents insist upon a bride's fee, a much larger payment paid by the groom. Lek's mother did not want the bride's fee. The ghost fee was sufficient and Adam happily agreed.

Adam and Lek did not have a large wedding celebration. Only a few of the village elders attended. But they did follow Khamu tradition. A special wedding rope was prepared by sewing together several strands of pure cotton. Once the rope was ready, it was blessed, and then tied around the hands of the two lovers. Khamu believe that the wedding rope will keep the couple together forever, and will permanently bind them to the Khamu family and community. Lek satisfied one flame; it was the other one, her burning desire to help elephants that needed more attention.

After the wedding, the couple began to plan a business future together. The laundry business was soon replaced with a tourist travel venture. Lek had worked as a tour guide and knew a little about the business. There were schools that trained people in the travel agency business, but Mr. and Mrs. Adam Chailert never went to such a school. Starting with just one table and a beat-up old typewriter, Lek and Adam began what would eventually become Gem Travel. They learned by doing and they learned by making mistakes. Renting office space from a Chinese landlord in Chiang Mai, the two of them quickly learned the ropes. Lek would call the airlines and make flight reservations for clients. At first she knew nothing about airline codes and would place the reservations under the client's name. When an airline got frustrated over her technique, she would convince whomever she was speaking with to reveal the code. She wrote it down and slowly, but slowly learned to book reservations like a "real" travel agent.

Lek brought many family members to Chiang Mai to help with her new business. She even arranged to have them attend a tour guide school. Soon, Gem Travel was taking up all of her time. Her great passion in life suffered as a result. She missed going to the jungle to help the elephants. The only way she could even see elephants was through her job, by attending tourist elephant camps. This only made things worse. At these camps she saw two very different sets of faces. On the faces of the tourists she saw great happiness as they laughed at tricks done by the elephants, or as they waited in line to ride an elephant. But for every trick they performed, Lek knew what these elephants had gone through. Many had passed through the awful crush. The natural love between a mother and her baby was beaten out of them. They suffered unimaginable pain. They bled to make tourists laugh. Now, as Lek watched, these magnificent creatures were forced to dance on cue, just as their mahouts trained them. It was this painful alternative that stung Lek deep inside her soul. Now, as a tour company operator, she was part of the problem.

Lek knew exactly what went on behind the scenes in the jungle where elephants were trained. The more she saw the tourist camps, the more she wanted to tell the tourists the truth. That's when a tiny kernel of an idea began to take shape. That's when she began to think of herself as a teacher and advocate for humane treatment of the animals. That's when she formed the very first plan to educate tourists about how elephants were trained, including lessons about the crush. It was a radical idea. In fact, given the popularity of elephant shows in Thailand, for Lek to tell her clients about the cruelty practiced on the animals bordered on insanity!

But that's exactly what she did. Whenever she had the chance, Lek told her tourist clientele how elephants were trained to do tricks. She did not hide anything. As time went on, more and more "trained" tourists questioned the mahouts at the elephant camps. Some were clearly unhappy when the elephants performed tricks. Others even showed anger toward the elephant camp employees, especially when they saw a mahout beat an elephant that did not do its trick properly.

Word soon spread. One elephant camp manager saw that tourists from Lek's travel agency complained the most, and some even refused to ride the elephants. A threatening phone call was made to one of Lek's tour guides: "Either control your clients or you will be banned from bringing them to the elephant camp."

Despite the trouble with the elephant camps, Lek and Adam were running a very successful business. Gem Travel was able to do more and more travel-related activities. Starting with little more than three hundred dollars, they grew their business into one of the best companies in Chiang Mai, booking flights, including international flights, hotel reservations, car rentals, and tours. Adam used his command of English to create tour brochures. Lek helped make the tour maps. Little by little, things came together. They bought a motorcycle so they could pick up tickets as soon as they were ready. The business was going so well that Lek created sub-agents who referred clients to Gem Travel tours for a commission.

Once the business was running smoothly, Lek told Adam she needed to go back home, home to the jungle. Something was calling her. She promised Adam she would not be gone long. Her husband did not like it. Her family, now part of the travel agency, did not understand why she had to leave. But for Lek, something was haunting her, tugging at her very soul.

Logging had been outlawed. More and more mahouts were out of a job. The Karen people, once in charge of so many elephants, were suffering. Lek had worked with the elephant people of northern Thailand and Burma for years. She could feel their pain, just as she could feel the pain of the elephants. Despite the wishes of her husband and of her family, she headed back to the jungle. She discovered hill tribe people, people just like her, desperately struggling to make ends meet.

When Lek returned to the jungle she saw an amazing sight. Huge trees had been cut down and were just rotting on the ground. In addition, the government had ordered thousands upon thousands of acres of jungle forest burned to make room for fruit tree crops, the new moneymaker according to the Thai government. The government supplied the young trees at no cost if the Karen hill tribe people living in the area would plant them and harvest the fruit.

At night Lek could look up at the mountains surrounding Baan Lao and see a vast ocean of fire. But it meant much more than clearing the land for a new crop. It meant that elephants were no longer necessary as beasts of burden. The logging ban made sure of that. Raising them had become a financial burden. Lek saw how underfed the elephants had become. Many mahouts sold their elephants to make ends meet. Families with sick children could not afford medicine. Some mahouts traveled deep into the jungle to work at illegal logging camps, hidden from government officials. The fire Lek saw was destroying more than trees. It was destroying a way of life. How could she help? How could one Khamu village girl now in business in the city help these people? That's what Lek faced when she went back home. On her second night in the village, these questions only became more urgent as nearly thirty mahouts from the entire region converged on Lek. They came seeking Lek's help.

Fire, Blood, and Bullets

It would be a long time before Lek could even begin to answer the desperate cries of the mahouts displaced by the jungle fire. Eighteen months after the fire, Lek met someone who could help. Through her company's many contacts in northern

Thailand, Lek met a businessman named Mr. N. She did not know exactly what business he ran, just that he had a lot of money and a passion for elephants. When he told Lek that he wanted to start an elephant camp for tourists, her heart nearly exploded with excitement. He wanted Lek's advice since she was the area's recognized elephant expert. Just when her work with elephants seemed to be overtaken by events, someone with considerable wealth was about to send her back to the world she loved so much.

Lek agreed to help Mr. N. create a tourist camp. He would need many elephants. Lek could get them. That part would be easy, and it would mean she could help the mahouts who needed work so badly. She would supply all elephants and mahouts. But before she would, Lek told Mr. N. that there were two conditions that he must agree to before she would help him. First, he must agree to respect the hill tribe mahouts he employed at his new tourist camp. Some very unscrupulous business owners forced their workers to work long hours at tiny wages. Then, they found ways to charge the employees for ridiculous services, reducing their pay even more. Lek's condition would prevent this. It also meant that his mahouts would be released from work to attend hill tribe ceremonies and special occasions. Mr. N. agreed.

The second condition concerned the elephants themselves. Even though this was to be a tourist attraction, Lek would only agree to help him if he promised humane treatment for the elephants she supplied. Humane treatment meant that there would be no tricks. It also meant that the elephants would be properly fed and released to the jungle at night so they could roam and forage, and be as free as possible. Mr. N. agreed to her second demand.

Even though Lek did not own an elephant park at the time, her work with the animals was known throughout the region. Her expertise was widely respected by the hill tribe people, especially the Karen who owned many elephants. This expertise did not come from any one source. For many of her herbal cures she could certainly credit her grandfather and the days spent under his tutelage as the "little doctor." But over the years she specialized in elephants, in their diet and in curing their ills. She did this after spending years watching them.

Mr. N. found a large plot of land next to a small river. Lek thought it was the perfect place to build the camp. The river was critical to ensure that the elephants could get enough water into their gigantic stomachs and as a source for bathing. Like humans, elephants need fresh air and places where social interaction can take place. Elephants thrive on river habitats. In the middle of Mr. N.'s land, a large bamboo hut surrounded by a viewing platform was constructed. From the platform, tourists could see and touch the elephants.

With Lek arranging for the elephants and their mahouts, Mr. N. needed just one thing more: customers! Lek's company sent twenty tourists to the camp on opening day. Her guides had to work hard to explain to the visitors that they would not be seeing an elephant "show." Instead, this would be a different kind of attraction, one that would teach them about the beautiful creatures. No one knew, not even Lek, if this would work. Would people from other lands pay to learn about elephants instead of riding them, or watching them dance or paint?

On the one hand, Mr. N. risked losing money for lack of customer support. On the other hand, a new risk arose if his camp proved successful. No other company at the time brought tourists to learn about elephants. Mr. N.'s competitors ran traditional tourist sites complete with elephant rides and elephant tricks. If Lek's humane treatment approach won over customers, this would mean less business for the other camps. That would spur jealousy and anger from the rival camps.

Gem Travel sent more and more tourists to the new camp. With Lek's hard work, it was becoming a very successful operation. Lek received a bizarre measure of the new camp's popularity. One of the rival elephant camp owners threatened one of Lek's tour guides. The same man left a message for Lek, ordering her to meet with him. Lek refused, not out of fear, but because she had done nothing wrong. If anything, the rival camp owner was in the wrong for threatening her and her guide, and for letting the elephants of his camp suffer abuse.

Other strange events occurred. An official from the Department of Forestry paid a visit to Mr. N.'s camp. He inspected the premises. He looked at the paperwork Mr. N. filed with the government. Everything seemed to be in order. A short

The Elephant Lady of Thailand

time later, police showed up claiming the camp structures were made of timber from an illegal logging company. Mr. N. was jailed for a brief time, and then forced to fight the action in court.

Things got so bad that Lek refused to take any tourists to the rival camps. During peak tourist season she was sending up to one hundred clients a day to Mr. N.'s elephant-friendly camp. In the fall of 1994 the real nightmare began. A large group of intruders attacked Mr. N.'s camp, setting fire to the buildings. The main building was burned to the ground. Mr. N. had built a restaurant on the premises and this, along with several smaller huts, was destroyed by fire.

At first, it looked as if the only camp interested in the well-being of the animals was out of business. But something amazing followed. As more and more travel agencies heard about the fire, they sent more and more of their clients to Mr. N.'s camp. It was much more difficult to teach people with the damage from the fire. Feeding visitors with no restaurant was also a challenge. Miraculously, the camp survived. People really did want to learn about elephants. Unfortunately, the concept of a place where elephants were loved and cared for went against the profit motive of the other elephant camps, so more trouble followed.

Mr. N. was able to quickly rebuild his camp. In a very short time he had twenty elephants. It was December 25, 1994, Christmas Day in some parts of the world, when two of his elephants became violently ill. There was no advance indication of illness or disease. The elephants started vomiting. They fell to the ground, rolling their huge bodies in agony. The only explanation for their sudden death was that someone had poisoned them. The Karen mahouts panicked. Many took their elephants and fled the camp. Twenty elephants soon dwindled to nine.

Mr. N. was faced with disaster. Tour companies did not want to send their clients to his camp now. There weren't enough elephants. If elephants were being poisoned, could humans be targeted next? Yet, Mr. N. would not give in. He visited all of the travel agencies in the area. He promised them that he would quickly restock his camp with more elephants. Once again they responded, saving his camp as it stood on the brink of failure.

With Lek's help, he threw a large thank-you dinner for the companies. Things seemed to be improving. In the face of phone threats, fire, and poison, Mr. N.'s elephant-friendly tourist camp kept going. It seemed like it was meant to be. Perhaps Lek's radical idea was destined to take root. It seemed as if nothing could stop it.

In early January, 1995, Lek received an anonymous phone call. The stranger warned her to stay away from Mr. N. Under no circumstances was she to ride with him in the same car. She told Mr. N. about the call. He laughed it off. Someone was out to scare them, he told her. The rival camps were trying to drive Lek away from her friend. Toward the end of January, one of Lek's friends was scheduled to visit from England. Lek told Mr. N. that she wanted her friend to see the elephant camp. Mr. N. offered to drive them, but Lek had already arranged for a car driven by her brother.

In the early morning hours of January 29, Lek had a very strange dream. Mr. N. walked into her house. That in itself wasn't so strange, but he walked through the door of the house without opening it! She woke up in a fright. She ran down to the first floor to call him and warn him again. When she did, she found Mr. N. waiting there for her. He had come to drive her and her English friend to the camp. Lek politely explained that her brother would be driving, and that they had planned on stopping at another tourist site that day. Mr. N. understood, but still insisted on leading the way to the camp in his car.

Lek's party set out for the camp, following Mr. N.'s vehicle. After stopping once for gas, Mr. N.'s vehicle proceeded on, ahead of Lek's car by a few minutes. Lek's brother soon followed, coming to an area surrounded by thick jungle. They were only a few hundred feet from the elephant camp when they spotted Mr. N.'s car stopped in the middle of the road. Something was wrong. The car's emergency lights were flashing.

Lek could see a man's head hanging out of the driver's door. It was Mr. N. Blood was coming out of his mouth and nose. It was a frightening scene. Lek told her brother to pull over. When he did, Lek jumped out to help the bleeding man. As she neared Mr. N.'s car, she saw that the windows were shot out. The car had been riddled with bullets. She shouted to her brother to turn their car around. They were in the crossfire, trapped behind Mr. N.'s car.

Despite the danger, Lek ran to Mr. N. She found him near death, bleeding uncontrollably. As weak as he was, he tried to tell Lek something, moving his lips but Lek could not make out any words. Then Lek saw something even more horrifying than the blood. Mr. N.'s arm was completely cut off or blown off.

After her brother turned their car around so they could escape, he jumped out to help Lek. Mr. N. uttered very few audible words. Lek could barely understand him, but realized he was trying to tell her about his children, his two babies. He wanted Lek to help his wife take care of them. As he lay bleeding to death, he was trying with the strength he still had to make a dying declaration.

After getting out these words about his family, Mr. N. said he was cold. He mumbled that he was very tired and needed to sleep. Lek shouted at him not to sleep. By now, the blood had soaked through Lek's shirt. She did not want him to pass out. She thought if he did he would surely die. Lek and her brother carried him to their car, laying him on the back seat. Her British friend sat stunned, frozen to his seat, shocked at what was happening. Before they sped away, away from the danger and toward medical help, Lek had to make one more trip to the shot-out car. She had to try to find Mr. N.'s arm.

It was a surreal scene. Lek sat in the back seat with Mr. N. Everything was soaked in his blood. Lek sat there tending to her friend, clutching his severed arm.

They drove to the nearest medical facility, but it was only a small clinic with no means to perform surgery. Only major surgery could save the man. A van took Mr. N. from the clinic to the hospital. Blood was given intravenously as he lay in the van. Lek, her brother, and their guest from abroad followed in their car.

This was not the first attack of its kind. Making money from tourist elephant camps was a serious business in northern Thailand. Not long before the attack on Mr. N., an elephant camp owner and his girlfriend had been kidnapped from their apartment. Three days after they disappeared, their charred remains were found inside their own car. Police suspected it was the work of a rival camp, but no arrests were made.

At the hospital someone had to sign a consent form before the doctors would operate. Mr. N.'s wife was over four hundred miles away. Lek was able to call her and get her permission to sign on her behalf. It was a very confusing scene, with Mr. N. missing his arm, doctors waiting to operate, and Lek's clothes soaked with blood now caking and smelling like death.

Even more bizarre, the doctors ushered Lek into the operating room to watch. She watched as they cut into his chest with a special machine. Blood seemed to be everywhere. She had grown up around blood. Chickens and pigs were slaughtered for meals. Elephants were seriously injured. But nothing could compare to the blood she saw coming from Mr. N. The operation was exploratory, looking for bullet wounds and bullets. It took nearly five hours. Before the doctors were finished, Lek became sick to her stomach and had to leave the operating room.

The attempted murder of Mr. N. was heavily covered by the local news media. Reporters from newspapers and television stations were sitting in the waiting room. The news from the murder of the other elephant camp owner and his girlfriend was still fresh, so this shooting only fed the media buzz. It was beginning to look like elephant camp wars had broken out. Before Lek had time to think, someone was pushing a microphone in her face, asking her what happened. But the police also wanted to know what happened. A police officer advised her not to speak to the news media until she provided an official statement for the police investigation.

The investigation proved efficient and successful. In a very short time, police identified the gunman. Through him they determined that the attack was arranged by one of the rival elephant camps in the area. The camp manager and his entire team were arrested and thrown in jail.

Amazingly, Mr. N. lived through the ordeal. Despite the loss of blood and the severed arm, he recovered after spending several weeks in the hospital. His arm was successfully reattached. However, the publicity about the vicious attack was not good for him. Unknown to Lek, he had many unhappy customers and business partners from his other "business interests" who now could find him. To Lek, he and his wife were kind people who genuinely loved elephants. But he was apparently connected to a sinister element. Once he made all the newspapers and the story of the attack was played again and again on the television stations, he became the most recognizable man in northern Thailand. Men with scores to settle lined up to get him. Mr. N. soon disappeared from the area.

The Birth and Death of Love

The loss of Mr. N. from the scene created chaos and a panic. The elephants and mahouts brought in for the elephant-friendly camp, the one Lek put her reputation behind, now had nowhere to go. The camp no longer had an owner. It could not operate without someone to pay the bills. As soon as the mahouts realized what had happened, they turned to the only person they trusted. They turned to Lek, not knowing what she could do, and not knowing what would happen to their families. Some were already thinking about taking their elephants and heading deep into the jungle, to the illegal logging camps. That seemed to be the only way to continue to earn a living.

Lek did not know what to do. So many people and animals were depending upon her. Not only the mahouts she brought in for Mr. N.'s elephant camp, but her employees at Gem Travel. Then there was Adam. Last and certainly not least in her mind were the elephants that came with the mahouts. Whatever she decided, some would be happy and others, well, Lek simply did not know.

What Lek could not deny was her intense, very real love for elephants. She was born with this love. No matter where life took her, from eking out a living through her laundry business and now through her travel agency, that deep love was never ever far from her heart, mind, and soul. In the aftermath of the attack on Mr. N., Lek and Adam set in motion a plan that would lead to a new beginning to nurture that love. It would also go a long way in destroying their marriage.

Within six months of the attack, Adam and Lek had a name for the new venture. They would create a new elephant camp, one modeled after the one Lek designed for Mr. N. They would call it Elephant Nature Park. After deciding on the name, the first real obstacle was finding suitable land. Lek found land not far from Mr. N.'s camp. A river ran through it, making it a good elephant habitat, perfect for bathing, drinking, and socializing. But buying it would be difficult.

Three separate families owned the land. Lek had to negotiate the terms with all three. She explained how she would use the land, to save and protect abused elephants, hoping this would appeal to the owners' sense of decency, and bring the price down. Forty-four acres would cost over thirty thousand U.S. dollars, or well over a million Thai baht. Lek had nowhere near that amount. It seemed impossible. She visited the elephants and mahouts nearby, at the elephant camp Mr. N. had founded. She felt very guilty. It was her word and her two special conditions that had brought the men and their animals here. Now, instead of protecting them and the elephants, the mahouts were unemployed and the future looked worse than ever.

It may have been the craziest time of Lek's life. The sensible thing to do was to save more money, money earned through Gem Travel, while continuing to look for land bargains. But Lek was a stubborn and impatient hill tribe woman. She would not wait. The elephants needed a permanent home. There were more elephants out there that needed the same. Yet, the only thing she and Adam had was a name. Elephant Nature Park was more of a dream than a reality. Lek chose to act on her dream. The three landowners agreed to a down payment and full payment of the balance three months later. Lek began to sell off her other possessions to find the money. She was able to come up with a down payment equivalent to nearly seven thousand U. S. dollars.

Lek owned a small piece of land and a house, dating back to her university days. She had paid off enough of the loan so that she could make a nice profit on the sale of both. She told the owners of the new land she would sell it to help pay the remainder. They agreed to let her start working the land immediately. It was all definitely insane. To make her dream come true, Lek was selling all of her worldly possessions and using every bit of the profit from the travel agency.

Lek called upon her family to help her start Elephant Nature Park. Not everyone was excited by the project. The brutal attack on Mr. N. shocked Lek's mother, Phong Sri. Boonta, the oldest, did not want to be part of such a dangerous enterprise. As Lek was putting together the building blocks that would launch her dream, the son of a nearby elephant camp owner and his wife were kidnapped. Both were later found—murdered. Fear was an honest and powerful influence on Boonta and Phong Sri. Boonta went so far as to tell Lek that her elephant venture put the whole family at risk. He was also thinking of his own family—of his wife and his son. Boonta traveled back to Baan Lao to ask Phong Sri to talk with Lek and ask her to abandon the elephant project.

Phong Sri met with Lek. She told her how she and Boonta thought the plan was just too dangerous. Lek listened obediently, but she would not change her mind. She told her mother that she would open a camp that would not take business away from other camps. She promised to visit all of the nearby camps and explain this to the owners. Above all, she told Phong Sri that she felt it her responsibility to take care of the mahouts who once worked for Mr. N. While accepting her daughter's words, Phong Sri continued to worry about her daughter's safety. Boonta refused to ride in the same car as Lek.

Lek depended on her family to help her with the incredibly difficult task of opening a new elephant camp. But with Boonta's continuing protest, and with two sisters who left Thailand after marrying foreigners, only two siblings remained to help Adam and Lek start a new camp. With them and the mahouts, Lek had a small but very determined work crew. Adam was very supportive at the outset. He managed the Elephant Nature Park office and wrote brochures in English that would be sent to area travel agencies. The really hard, physical part was working the land, and converting raw jungle and old rice paddies into a true nature park. Huts had to be constructed to house the mahouts. A central lodge was needed so tourists could congregate at a central location, learn about the elephants, and see the elephants up close.

Working the land was a backbreaking exercise. This had been a rice field, meaning very flat land with virtually no trees. Lek and her crew planted dozens upon dozens of trees. They had to do all of the landscaping. This included bringing in tons of topsoil to raise the level of depressed areas. They also built a road to connect the outside world to this land, and smaller roads inside the park to connect the various huts.

The huts themselves were major projects. The mahouts needed shelter immediately, so these took priority. After that, a large hut housing the park's center was built, where the office would be located, and where tourists could congregate.

Lek, her husband, family members, and a family of mahouts completed the basic construction of Elephant Nature Park. Now it was a reality. In short order, the mahouts and nine elephants moved into their new "home." It all seemed so wonderful, at least in Lek's mind. But almost from the day the park opened, problems began. The cost of running the operation used up more and more of Lek and Adam's money. More and more money made from the travel business had to be channeled into the nature park to make ends meet.

The financial problem was huge, yet Lek was uncompromising. She refused to abandon her principles for quick profit. This was to be a humane elephant park. There would be no elephant rides or elephants for trekking through the jungle. She would not allow the elephant tricks that many tourists would have gladly paid to see. She established essentially the same rules she required Mr. N. to follow for her own elephant camp operation. If anything, her rules for the nature park mahouts were stricter. They were not allowed to use hooks or anything to inflict pain upon their animals. When elephants became ill, they would not be forced to work. When they became too old, they must be released into the jungle. Every mahout had to understand that this place was different. It was founded on the principles that humans must respect elephants and everyone must strive to live together in harmony.

Word spread quickly about the new elephant park. It was a different kind of tourist spot. Different made it very attractive. Travel agents who had sent tourists to Mr. N.'s elephant camp, now wanted to try the new place. Soon after the park became fully operational, in 1996, the tourists began arriving in large numbers.

But even the initial popularity did not relieve Lek of the financial pressure. The money that Elephant Nature Park took in during its opening months all went to feeding the elephants and paying the mahouts. Lek had to spend most of her time working on the grounds of the park, trying to make it a showcase, literally trapped there with so much work to do each day. She taught her paying customers about elephants. She stretched the budget so her employees could get paid. There were so many things to take care of, so many details, and so much work still left to do. Soon the operation began to consume her. Something had to suffer. She suffered through the tiring days. But the real strain from such a large operation became the strain she and Adam felt on their marriage.

Adam and Lek began the new venture together. The worsening money situation began to place a great deal of stress upon them individually and upon the marriage itself. Adam looked forward to buying a house and starting a family with Lek. But all of their money seemed to be needed, not for a house, but for the new elephant park. At first, Lek tried to keep their marriage together. Each morning before she went to the park, she would prepare meals for Adam and store them in the refrigerator, ready whenever he needed them. But she noticed more and more he wasn't touching the food. He spent most of his time away from her and increasingly with his own friends.

Lek made good progress with Elephant Nature Park. In less than two years, a steady flow of tourists streamed into the park. In that time, the necessary huts were built, along with elephant shelters and even a bamboo hut used to serve lunch to the visitors. Other business people in the area were so impressed that Lek received a number of offers. Some wanted to be her business partner. Others wished to invest in the park. But she refused them all. Her fear was that they were driven only by the desire to make money and not as she was, by a deep commitment to take care of elephants. If she had a partner only interested in a large profit, soon elephant tricks would be introduced. All of her work would be for nothing. Lek would not let this happen.

While conditions at Elephant Nature Park continued to improve, the entire business venture drained all of Adam and Lek's money. The two reached a new low in their marriage. In 1997, Adam's grandmother passed away. He and Lek could not find enough money for a plane ticket so he could attend the funeral in England. Lek slipped to a new low point in her life. It wasn't the same feeling as when that truck slid down the mountain and onlookers said not to worry because if she died she was "just a Khamu." That was a horrible time too, but she was just a young girl. This was a new kind of low. Not so much shame for being so worthless, but guilt for being helpless. It was a very real, very large guilt. Against all of the advice of other family members, and in the face of mounting financial debt, Lek pressed ahead with her park. Now the man she loved had to suffer. The start of the elephant park should have been a time of great happiness and adventure. Instead, it was the beginning of a long period of challenges and suffering.

Phong Sri's Dream Comes True

As her first try at building a unique home for elephants began to fail, another, even more challenging problem appeared in Lek's life. Her mother's health began to fail. Lek's mother had always been the anchor in her life, the one person she could count on to help her stay focused on her life's mission. Grandfather Noom taught her herbal cures. He taught her to always respect the spirit of the jungle. But Phong Sri stood by her through all her trials, whether they involved money or marriage. Phong Sri was her angel.

As her troubles mounted, Lek thought of her mother. The new elephant park was sapping Lek's energy. Her marriage was falling apart. She had to find her center again. She returned to her childhood home of Baan Lao. More importantly, she needed her mother's love and guidance to give her strength. The new park was a refuge for elephants, but Baan Lao was her own sanctuary. Her mother's house was her own personal refuge.

When Lek arrived, she was surprised to see how much weight her mother had lost. There was no telephone in the village, so the only way for the two to communicate was by letter. But her mother did not warn her even by mail that things had turned so bad. Phong Sri was worried that if her daughter knew about her illness, this might interfere with Lek's work with elephants. When she returned to Baan Lao, Lek soon discovered the truth. Her mother was in a lot of pain and did not know why. Despite her mother's insistence that she did not need a doctor,

Lek took her to the local hospital. The diagnosis was not bad, but the cure would be painful. Phong Sri was suffering from a kidney stone that would not pass. She needed an operation, but the doctor told Lek her mother would have to wait a month since several others were ahead of her.

Lek could see this would be a month of terrible pain, so she began looking for other hospitals. She found one with only a two-week wait, but that still was too long for Lek. Eventually, she agreed to pay more to get her mother in right away. This included a private room that cost a small fortune at a thousand baht per day, or nearly thirty U.S. dollars per day. Phong Sri underwent the surgery. As she lay in bed recuperating, her family visited. Lek and her siblings went up to their sleeping mother, just to kiss her or hold her hand. Once the doctors released her from the hospital, Lek and her sister, Wasana, took Phong Sri back to Baan Lao to nurse her back to health.

Several months went by. The pain returned but the diagnosis was not as simple as a kidney stone that would not pass. One of Phong Sri's kidneys was failing completely. She had to undergo a blood transfusion, more tests, and treatment on the kidney that still functioned. She could no longer hold her food down. Her skin was turning yellow.

Six of Phong Sri's seven children came to the hospital to see her through. Only Phetrin who lived in the United States was not there. As the doctors came and went, Phong Sri asked each child how much her treatments were costing the family. Lek paid the bills, and after much questioning by her sick mother, she finally told her. Her mother was shocked. She could only think of how many more elephants Lek could help with that money. She was absolutely beside herself over the financial burden she caused for her daughter.

One day Lek left the hospital for a few hours to attend to business at the elephant park. When she returned, her mother's bed was empty. In a panic she set about to find her. No one at the nurses station knew where she was. Crazy and frightening thoughts ran through Lek's head. Was she dead? Did she have a relapse? Lek looked in the physical therapy room to no avail. Then, she began a room-to-room search. After some very tense moments, a nurse found her mother on a nearby balcony. She had forced herself to get up, out of bed, and walk to the balcony. There she was trying to stretch her body in exercise. She told Lek that she would get better so Lek would not have to pay any more for her hospital stay. If she did that, she knew Lek could do more for the elephants who needed her. It was an amazing act of love.

Over the next several weeks her mother's condition worsened. Lek began to fear that her angel was about to leave her. She decided she must honor her mother. She had a new, larger house built for her. It was one of the nicest in Baan Lao. She also arranged something very special, something that she knew her mother wanted very badly. Like millions of other Thai citizens, her mother revered the royal family. She told Lek that if she could just meet a member of this family, she could close her eyes and die a happy woman.

Lek contacted the provincial governor of Chiang Mai. She asked if the royal family could be invited to the area. The governor had good news. The first daughter of the king, her Royal Highness, Princess Ubonrat, was scheduled to visit Chiang Mai soon. Lek persuaded the governor to arrange for a stop at the elephant park.

On the day of the visit Phong Sri dressed up as she never had. The entire local community was filled with excitement. People from nearby mountain villages trekked down in the hopes of catching a glimpse of this very special visitor. Over a thousand found a way down mountain roads to the elephant park. Lek's own Khamu hill tribe people came too.

Lek's family was allowed to stand near the government officials, close to the route of the princess and her entourage. The men assigned to provide security made all other onlookers stand at a distance. When Phong Sri saw what was happening, she asked her daughter if the elderly village people could come and stand with her. She knew many of these had walked several miles just for a chance to see the princess. When the governor granted this, several of the elderly Khamu men and women joined Phong Sri.

Lek's mother was chosen to give flowers to Princess Ubonrat. The princess was gracious, stopping to ask her about her health. She was given a tour of the elephant park. Phong Sri was so nervous at seeing Princess Ubonrat that she became sick to her stomach. After the princess left her area, she vomited uncontrollably. After the special visit was over, she was taken back to the hospital. There she slept a very sound and long sleep, something she had not done in a long while. When she awoke, her appetite was back and she was anxious to start therapy and daily exercise. The visit by the royal highness seemed to be a wonder cure.

Lek's Nightmare Comes True

Lek spent much less time helping elephants while her mother's health was in decline. She spent many months in Baan Lao or in the hospital caring for Phong Sri. When her health seemed to be improving, especially after the royal visit, Lek resumed her work. It was while her mother remained hospitalized that Lek received a call that an elephant had been shot. Even with her mother's improvement, she did not want to leave her side. Her greatest fear was that she would leave and return too late—too late to say a final goodbye. When her mother heard the news that an elephant was in distress, she begged her daughter to leave.

"Look at me," she said. "I am surrounded by doctors; that elephant only has you."

Lek decided to go. Her mother gave her a special Buddha necklace for good luck, known as a survival amulet. After leaving Phong Sri's bedside, Lek put together a rescue team, a so-called *jumbo express*, for the elephant suffering from a gunshot wound. The wounded elephant was in a distant jungle, hard to get to, and made more difficult by the rainy season. Her team traveled by truck, heading up a tall mountain. Heavy rains turned the only road into deep mud before they could get close to the village. They had to leave the truck with the driver and continue on foot, up jungle trails.

After an extremely difficult trek to the village, Lek and her team successfully treated the elephant. They spent the night in the village. The next day they hiked down the mountain. When they reached the stranded truck, a police officer was standing next to the driver. This was not a good sign. The first thing that came to Lek's mind was that her mother had died. The policeman told her that her mother had slipped into a coma and she needed to return as soon as possible. There was more bad news. The road was buried by a mudslide. They were forced to walk back through the jungle. The policeman advised them to follow the river since it led to the elephant park. That meant literally cutting their way through thick undergrowth and clusters of river bamboo.

In the face of such terrible news, Lek and her team began to cut large bamboo stalks. They would construct a raft. It took hours just to finish the raft. The whole time Lek's head was spinning with grief. The only way to get back in less than a day was to raft down the river to the elephant park. Even at this, it was a perilous twelve-hour journey in the rain.

It was during this arduous trek that Lek began to beg. She begged the spirits to take her life—to let her trade places with her mother—if only they would let her mother live. It was one of the most desperate moments of her life. The going was extremely slow and treacherous. Rain was pelting down on the raft. All Lek could think about was her dying mother. During the twelve hours on the river, she would sit on a corner of the raft, unfazed by the horrible conditions, and cry. Her tears and the rain seemed to be endless.

She cried through the terrible weather, "Please Mother, wait for me! I look forward to seeing you. Don't leave me!" She prayed with these thoughts as the raft bounced through the churning river. In desperation, she yelled to the spirits, "If my mother has died, then I want the river to take me now!"

When she reached her mother, Phong Sri was in a deep sleep, unable to communicate. Lek was too late. She obeyed her mother's wishes and left her to help an elephant. The forces of nature seemed to team up to slow her return. All she found after her difficult journey and after so many prayers was a mother unable to speak and about to die. Lek sat next to her looking deep into her eyes. She was heartbroken. In reality, her mother was gone. She felt abandoned. The survival Buddha abandoned her. The jungle spirits did not answer her cries. She sat there holding her mother's hand, her eyes fixed on her mother's motionless face when Phong Sri startled her. Her mother opened her eyes!

Her mother began to move, to agitate, and to shake as if her body was going through its final spastic motions of a dying woman. But soon Lek learned that a miracle was unfolding. Her mother had not died. The coma had not stolen her away. Her mother was motioning with her hands. She struggled to speak, but her tracheal tube made it nearly impossible. She made little swirling motions with both hands. Sounds came from deep down her throat. Lek tried to put the sounds and motions together.

Lek finally understood her: "Pen—pen. Give me a pen!" She gave her mother a pen and helped her write out her thoughts. Phong Sri wrote something down, something short but powerful: "I love you."

They were the most beautiful words Lek ever saw. Mother and daughter were still united in life by this great, great love. Through her misery and pain, from failed kidneys, and through the dark veil of a coma, Phong Sri returned to tell Lek she loved her.

She wrote more: "Stand like a rock!"

Her mother was telling her to keep faith with her calling. She must not let other people or other events take her away from the elephants. As her writing caused a stir in the hospital, the tracheal tube was removed. After that Phong Sri spoke nonstop for the next twelve hours.

She talked about many things. She even spoke English, something Lek never knew her to do. She was speaking to both Lek and Adam when she did, telling them that love can cause pain. She was talking about their broken marriage. She told her daughter to get away from the pain and make her proud. At one point she said, "I don't want to die because I have such a beautiful daughter."

It was an amazing sight to Lek and her family. Phong Sri never spoke so openly before. She found something to say about everyone. She even questioned her husband's faithfulness. Lek was shocked at the words because her mother always taught the children they must never, ever show disrespect toward him.

As wonderful as it was to hear her mother again, it did not last. Phong Sri slipped back into the in-between zone, somewhere between awareness and death. The family quickly realized the end must be near. One of Lek's sisters went to a fortuneteller, looking for a miracle. Hundreds of candles were lit in the nearby Buddhist temple to honor their sick mother. Phong Sri fell into a deep sleep. Lek sat by her side, dedicated with love to the last.

As Lek stood watch over her dying mother, she thought about her childhood. She remembered how hard it was to fall asleep in her tiny bedroom in Baan Lao. The nights were hot and filled with the sounds of the jungle. But her "angel" was always there. Her mother sung the children to sleep.

Now Lek would sing her mother to sleep. Now she would repay her, even if this sleep was going to last forever. Mother and daughter touched each other for the last time. Lek sang to Phong Sri through tears. She sang one of the sweet lullabies of her childhood. She held her mother's hands and sang to her, close to her face, so the words fell on Phong Sri like sweet kisses. She would not wake again. She was just sixty-two.

With the death of her mother in late 1998, dark clouds were forming. Elephant Nature Park, her dream refuge for elephants, begun three years earlier, was slipping out of her control. In order to finance the building of the park, she had to rely on money from other family members. While Lek embarked on elephant rescue missions, control of the park fell to her two sisters and their American spouses. The spouses used their own money to fund the day-to-day operation of the park. There was no common purpose between Lek and the family members who loaned her money. She wanted to save elephants; they wanted to make money from elephants.

Lek's family troubles did not end with her two sisters and their *farang* of westerner spouses. She was deeply hurt when her father began seeing another woman barely two weeks after Phong Sri passed away. Her father, Sa-Nguan, held the business license needed to run Elephant Nature Park. When he heard that Lek disapproved of his new arrangement, he signed the license over to yet another family member. The title to the land belonged to another sibling, a sister. She and Lek had a falling out when the sister began an affair with the husband of one of Lek's best friends. This led to the land being signed over to one of the

The Elephant Lady of Thailand

American in-laws. Within months of Phong-Sri's passing Lek had no say over the land or the business. At one point the disagreement became so sharp that Lek was banned from even entering the park she founded. The only thing she was able to retain was the name.

As the twentieth century came to a close, Lek had lost a great deal. Her marriage to Adam was crumbling. Her mother was dead. Her father turned his back on her. Siblings wrestled control out of her hands. This was the very elephant sanctuary she created! At the age of thirty-nine, what lay ahead seemed unclear. Her mother's deathbed counsel—"stand like a rock!"—seemed impossible. But no matter how terrible her personal life had become, there was always an elephant in need. There was always a reason to live.

Lek began to fear that her angel was about to leave her. She decided she must honor her mother. She had a new, larger house built for her. It was one of the nicest in Baan Lao.

The Spirit of Phong Sri: Elephant Haven

In the aftermath of her mother's death, Lek did not waste her time. Neither sadness nor a lack of money would stop her. In 1999, she set her sights on a mountaintop in the Mae Tang region north of Chiang Mai. The mountain was surrounded on all sides by lush jungle. It was an ideal world for elephants, not merely a place to recuperate in the presence of humans as they could in the nature park. This was a true elephant nature preserve, meant to maximize the freedom of these wonderful animals. Here, the elephants could walk for days without coming into contact with that other world, the one inhabited by human animals.

Lek knew the history of the land. She had been taking distressed and injured elephants there off and on since 1997. The government of Thailand owned it along with thousands of other acres in the region. Lek's mountaintop was a two-hour drive from Chiang Mai. For years the locals had used it for illegal logging. Lek wanted to use it for elephant rehabilitation. If R & R signified a rest and relaxation site for humans, this mountain represented a three-R habitat, devoted to rest, recuperation, and even reintegration back to nature.

In the months after her mother died, Lek spent more and more time at the elephant retreat. She paid rent to the local government for use of the land. She built a very primitive hut as her shelter. It took a while before the local inhabitants got used to seeing elephants in their jungle. Elephants frightened them. Elephants, they believed, could turn on them, killing them or seriously hurting them and their children. So it wasn't unexpected when they turned on Lek. Someone burned down Lek's hut, apparently hoping she would give up. She would not. It was burned down a second time. She rebuilt it again. *Stand like a rock* was still fresh in her mind. The hut she built that finally survived was tiny. It had no bedroom. It had no toilet. There was a small area for cooking.

Because of the turmoil in her family, Lek spent much of 1999 at the mountain. She planted new trees and tried to prevent the illegal loggers from destroying grown trees. She placed a piece of yellow cloth on the ones she wanted to save. She borrowed this from a monk's tradition. She placed a piece of cloth on each tree to make it immune from cutting. The cloth was symbolic of the robes worn by Buddhist monks. When passersby saw the cloth, they knew that these trees must not be cut down. To do so would be sacrilegious.[1] Lek took some

---

[1] In August 2002 an article appeared in a local magazine, *Good Morning Chiangmai News Magazine*, entitled "An Environmental Monk." It featured the senior monk of the very area where Elephant Haven was founded, the Mae Tang Valley. The monk

liberty with the custom in acting as an emissary for the temple. To her, the protection of Buddha was in harmony with the spirit of the jungle. Over the years, she and a small army of volunteers planted and saved thousands of trees.

One of Lek's supporters, Jennifer Hile, would produce an award-winning documentary based on her travels with Lek. Years after Lek created Elephant Haven, her friend described her work there and the amazing efforts to save the trees in the area:

"I spent much of that time [three months in Thailand and Burma observing elephant populations] with Lek Chailert, a Thai activist who devotes her life to throwing a shoulder against the downhill slide of these endangered animals. Lek owns a sanctuary called Elephant Heaven [Haven] where she takes in old and abused working elephants. It's the only free roaming sanctuary for elephants in Thailand. At her sanctuary, Buddhist monks gather in orange robes to wander through the forest, tying sacred cloths to the trees to protect them."[2]

Of course, it was Buddhist monks AND one elephant lady who worked to save the trees.

The elephants Lek took to the haven did their part. To ward off the loggers who liked to frequent the area, and perhaps discourage any more attempts to destroy her hut, Lek would let elephants stand guard. They stuck close to the hut and acted as a living shield for Lek and her volunteers. She was protected three ways. The spirit of her mother was always there. Monk's cloth protected the trees. And the elephants protected all. It was quite a triad of physical, spiritual, and motherly strength.

She was preparing this elephant retreat as nature therapy for abused elephants. She was keenly aware of the mental damage years of physical abuse did to elephants. Elephants possess an amazing mental awareness of what humans are doing to them. That's why their eyes are so expressive like Pang Boon Ma's soulless look of shock. To counter the effects of this, Lek created

---

explained how Buddhist beliefs were closely connected to nature, beliefs such as Dharma, the natural laws of truth, and Karma, the personal consequences of today's world influencing how one will be reincarnated in another life. The monk was on a crusade to save the jungle forest. He directed his fellow monks to wrap saffron cloths around the largest trees. The cloths were blessed and symbolically represented monks. Cutting them down would be against Dharma and create bad Karma.

[2] *National Geographic*, "Vanishing Giants" by Jennifer Hile, Artist's Statement.

a haven for them. In fact, she named the habitat Elephant Haven. Human control was minimized. Human schedules for feeding were nonexistent at the haven. The natural cycle of eating, preening, socializing, and sleeping was restored. And it was not just therapy for the animals. Given what she had been through, it was her own place of rehabilitation and mental therapy. It was therapy for Lek's damaged soul.

When she wasn't planting trees or working to improve Elephant Haven, Lek spent her time observing. She followed the elephants she rescued. In 1999, the population of Elephant Haven was small, just nine, so it was not difficult to watch them as they tried to return to their natural ways. She delighted in seeing them forage as they wandered freely through the jungle. She felt comfort watching them enjoy a relaxing mud bath in one of the many streams. As she and her trusted volunteers helped turn Elephant Haven back to nature, reversing at least some of the human damage done by years of illegal logging, the place became her dreamland. It really was a mental landscape as well as a physical refuge. It helped cure the sickest of the elephants she brought there. It helped cure her.

The Elephant Lady of Thailand

In fact, she named the habitat Elephant Haven. Human control was minimized. Human schedules for feeding were nonexistent at the Haven. The natural cycle of eating, preening, socializing, and sleeping was restored.

Dennis W. Shepherd

The Growing Rucksack of Hope: Jumbo Express

Trips into the jungle to help save a dying elephant, or to cure a sick one, began on a modest scale. The missions really began as throw-some-things-in-the-rucksack-and-go trips. Lek began them alone, or, at best, with an uncle or other family member agreeing to drive. That usually meant driving as far as the jungle roads lasted, then hiking the rest of the way.

Over time, as Lek's reputation grew, jungle villages with worker elephants came to call upon her more and more. As her resources and resourcefulness improved, she took more supplies along. The rucksack grew into a truckload, that had to be offloaded with hired porters who would carry the supplies through the jungle, up a mountain, down a river, with Lek leading the way.

As far back as 1992, Lek had been keeping a record of her trips into the jungle. She recorded vital statistics concerning her rucksack visits to the villages. She organized her trips around these recorded notes, that told her what the people needed most, what animals they had, and when her last visit occurred. She knew when an elephant was used in the tourist trekking industry and in the supposedly banned logging business.

The trips began as rescue missions for just the elephants, but they expanded into humanitarian missions for the villagers she visited. Her notes told her if there were special needs. Helping elephants was always her primary mission, but Lek never hesitated to use her skill or draw upon her supplies to help every animal, even the human kind. Through these rucksack missions, Lek knew where cancer sufferers lived and brought them food or medicine to ease their pain. When a village was in the midst of a dysentery outbreak, Lek was there. Anything she and her team could do to relieve suffering, Lek included in the express.

Her reputation grew. She received requests for assistance throughout northern Thailand. No matter how rough the terrain, Lek could get there. A motorized vehicle took her team as far as the roads lasted. Rivers were highways too, and Lek and her fellow rescue team members could build a bamboo raft in hours, then float through high waters, swirling eddies, and sometimes paddle and pole along still waters to their destination. The jungle rainforest could be imposing. When there were no trails or streams, the only way was to take out machetes and hack their way through, cutting a path through jungle foliage, webs of jungle vines, and through thick clusters of bamboo.

Each trip taught Lek more. Each mission became more effective and was run more efficiently than the one before. The rescue teams took on form. With time, they were organized in a standard way. In the early days of these rucksack missions of hope, finding a veterinarian to go along was difficult. Taking one eventually became a necessity, a requirement of each foray into the jungle. Lek was still the little doctor of the jungle, but she was also a believer in the power of modern drugs and medical techniques that helped cure elephants.

Lek's passion was always for her beloved elephants, but every trip into a mountain village revealed a host of other needs. Sickness in the villages usually presented the greatest threat to the children and the elderly. Villages far removed from large cities, buried in the jungle like Ghost Creek, could not get medical care and medical supplies except through the chance visits of people like Lek. She did her best to take much needed supplies to them. The list of required supplies for these visits included old clothes Lek collected from friends and relatives, medicine any way she could find them, food items not easily found in a jungle village, and seeds to help grow mountain gardens.

Lek and her team were welcomed miles before they ever reached the host village. She would spy one, two, and then more children standing on a hillside, or at the top of a mountain road. The children waved and yelled as the express approached. These missions took on a special name—Jumbo Express—a name that signified both elephants and urgency. In the early 1990s, Lek began these trips just to rescue elephants by curing illness or treating wounds. As she did, she became familiar with most of the mahouts and remembered the elephants they rode, cared for, and sometimes abused. As the Jumbo Express concept grew, she expanded her elephant rescues to a relationship with an entire village. She became so well known, she was treated like royalty. The village leader hosted her. By the mid-1990s, her visits were far more than rucksack missions. They touched the lives of many.

In 2006, the Jumbo Express was a standard part of Lek's Nature Park mission. International organizations and foreign volunteers sought her out. Not only did they expand to helping people, they went beyond the country's borders. Jumbo Expresses traveled to Burma, Surinam, and India. Schools, bridges, and temples were built or repaired by Lek's teams. In 2007 alone, over twenty Express projects took place.

A Jumbo Express Failure: Lek the Kidnapper

Boon Khum, a bull elephant, was trained to haul heavy logs for a logging company. He was an aging animal, about sixty years old. With a set of fully grown tusks, he looked magnificent. He was also extremely useful because with those tusks, he could lift huge logs up to a truck as efficiently as any forklift.

One day Boon's mahout chained him to a tree not far from a small creek. The mahout left to eat his midday meal followed by a short nap. A loud humming noise woke him. It was the sound of a power saw echoing through the jungle. When the mahout reached Boon Khum, ivory poachers were sawing off one of Boon's tusks. They had drugged the elephant so they could work without any resistance. Boon lay on his side shaking uncontrollably as if he had a sudden stroke. The mahout ran to his work hut and retrieved a shotgun. Then he ran back and confronted the poachers, firing a warning shot in the air. The men ran for their lives, taking the one tusk they finished cutting.

Boon lay there helpless, still under the influence of the drugs the poachers injected into his huge body. Blood ran everywhere. The power saw was used in an especially cruel way. To maximize the amount of ivory they poached, the men cut at the very point where the tusk joined his facial nerve center. This led to massive bleeding, and when the drugs wore off, agonizing pain for Boon.

When Boon's head finally cleared, the pain began. To make things worse, his mahout decided he had to cut off the other tusk so poachers would not come back for that one. The once proud bull was now a severely wounded and handicapped animal. The pride of sixty years was lost when he lost his tusks. The strength he enjoyed as the main logging elephant, stronger than any other, was gone.

As the days passed, Boon's condition grew worse. His face became swollen with infection from the poachers' act of stealing every inch of his tusk. Maggots infested the wound. The logging camp owner forced him to continue to haul logs. The pain was so intense that Boon would stop working periodically and beat his head against the nearest tree in frustration. After watching this go on, the owner decided to get rid of him. He sold Boon to another company, this time to a trekking company that took tourists on elephant rides in the jungle.

Without treatment of any kind, Boon's pain became unbearable. He lost weight. It became more and more difficult for him to bear the load of tourist passengers. Lumps from his infection formed on his back under the skin. When the saddle was fastened to him, more pain followed. When tourists sat in the saddle, the pain got worse again. Now, instead of pounding his head in frustration, he shook his load violently, throwing off any tourist sitting atop him. This only made his new owner angry. His mahout punished him by shooting him with a pellet gun. No one seemed to realize that, without treatment, Boon would never get better and was on his way to the grave.

It was only after Boon was abused and his condition ignored that Lek was asked to help. She put together more than one Jumbo Express team to treat Boon. But she warned Boon's owner, unless he let the animal rest, he would never heal. After her second trip, Lek knew that no one was following her advice. Each time she returned, she found new shotgun pellets to remove. Boon was still being saddled to take tourists. Rest meant less money for the owner so there was no rest. On her third trip Lek saw something that told her the abuse continued. She saw a clear wet line beneath his eyes, tears falling from Boon's face as he walked. The pain must have been incredibly intense to make the giant bull cry.

Lek Chailert, the tiny moonlight girl, would not let anything stop her from saving an elephant in distress. Not rebel forces operating in elephant country. Not the elephant's owner. Not even the law. In Boon's case, she decided to take matters into her own hands. She told the owner that she needed to take Boon Khum into the jungle for treatment. She brought her own mahout on this express. She paid Boon's mahout to let her take Boon without him. Then she did something only the bravest of elephant rescuers would ever think to do. She and her own mahout slipped away from the trekking camp with Boon and headed into the jungle. They did not stop there. There was no treatment there. Instead, they continued their journey for five days, up and down mountains, until they reached the elephant park. This was the only way Lek believed there was even a chance to save the great bull elephant.

The police were waiting for her when she entered the park. She hoped that she could rest Boon Khum so he could properly heal, and then return him. But the owner contacted the authorities. Lek was being charged with a crime. The owner filed charges against her for stealing his property. Things seemed to be upside down. The one who abused the elephant was now the victim in the eyes of the law. The one who saved the elephant was the criminal.

Lek tried to explain the entire situation to the police. She told them about the injuries to Boon Khum. She told them that two owners had not let him rest long enough to allow his wounds to heal. She told them about the pellet shots fired into his skin. But the police could not or would not help. They told her there was no animal abuse law in Thailand, so the owners could not be held responsible. Boon was the property of the owner and Lek took that property without permission. It was an open-and-shut case. Lek was going to be arrested.

Lek offered to negotiate with the owner and settle the case. The police allowed her to try. Lek proposed a small fine, but the owner calculated a daily fee for the days his elephant was away. In effect, he was charging Lek as if she had rented the elephant as a tourist. The amount was staggering and Lek had to depend on friends to help pay it. But pay it she did. Her incredible efforts to save Boon Khum were defeated by greed and by a country without a legal way of stopping animal abuse.

One-Woman Express: Lek Defends a Killer

Lek's elephant rescue network, beginning as quick rucksack trips into the jungle, grew into a vast helping hand stretching across the northern jungles of Thailand, into more troublesome places like Burma, Cambodia, and Vietnam. Expresses have visited Sri Lanka and Nepal. Her method of finding elephants in distress began as word-of-mouth and gradually evolved, spreading near and far as her reputation for compassion became known throughout Asia.

Lek learned about one case, however, not by word-of-mouth and not through her Jumbo Express network. She discovered it by listening to the radio. In fact, she overheard it listening to a police scanner. What she heard was so unusual and so compelling that she decided to travel as soon as she heard it. An elephant was about to be *executed*.

Lek heard a lot of activity on the police channel. Somebody was dead. Something was going to be killed. It was a tragedy that was about to get worse. She decided to drop everything and head to the distant village where all of this was happening. She left Adam in the middle of the night, telling him she had to go. The village was in a very remote part of Thailand. Adam did not approve. The two argued, but she could not wait. It wasn't the first time she left on bad terms with her husband. But this may have been the last. Her marriage would not survive much longer. The two had separated by 1998 and the final legal end was just waiting for the last straw.

When she got to the village she decided to investigate. She learned that an elephant killed its mahout so the police were asked to kill the elephant. Stories about rampaging elephants are not uncommon. So-called domesticated elephants, mainly circus elephants, reportedly "go berserk" for no reason. They break their bindings and run wild, injuring or even killing someone unlucky enough to be in their path. Lek knew all too well that for every elephant that acts like this, there is a human reason or a reason based upon natural animal instincts that explains what happens.

Soon after arriving in the village of the condemned elephant, an elephant named Phai Phet, Lek spoke first with the widow of the mahout who was killed. To Lek's surprise, she did not want the elephant killed. In fact, she begged Lek to stop the plan to kill Phai Phet. That alone told her that there was much more to the story than what she overheard on the police channel.

She learned that the "killer" elephant had two owners. The owners took turns working him in their logging camps. One owner worked him all day long. With very little rest, the other owner used Phai Phet at night. The lack of rest wore the poor animal down. He became extremely agitated in the face of any change. The drug he was fed to keep him awake did not help matters.

For logging elephants it was not unusual for the owners to work an elephant day and night. In fact, sometimes elephants were fed a drug to keep them working. Thailand is known for a particular drug popular among young people, a drug called *ya baa*, also known as yaa baa. The phrase means "crazy medicine." Ya baa comes in small orange tablets. It is an amphetamine, or speed. With just a few days use, it is powerfully addictive. In logging camps, it is fed to elephants to keep them awake at all hours. In one case, Lek had to break an elephant's addiction to ya baa.

One day Phai Phet got wedged between two trees and couldn't free himself. His mahout began hitting him, trying to force him out with painful blows. At some point, the elephant got free suddenly lunging forward. This sent his mahout tumbling off his back onto the ground below. Another mahout working nearby began to laugh. This infuriated Phai Phet's mahout. He grabbed an ax and hit the elephant squarely on the face with the blunt end. What happened next would seal Phai Phet's fate. When the ax smashed into his forehead the animal reacted instantly and instinctively, whipping its trunk to one side. The trunk slammed into the mahout with such force that he was thrown into a tree, killing him instantly.

The people in the area were afraid to approach Phai Phet. They believed he had gone mad. They thought he was a killer elephant. But what this giant did next told Lek that it was an accident, an accident caused by the brutality of the mahout. Phai

Phet began poking and nudging his mahout. He did not know he was dead. His instincts told him the mahout was sleeping, so he carefully guarded the body, waiting for his master to wake up. Lek also discovered that at one point Phai Phet carried the body down to the river and washed it. When he could get no response from his mahout, the elephant began to moan in sadness.

It was because Lek found out the truth that this "killer" lived. When the villagers learned that it was an instinctual reaction brought on by great pain, and that the wife of the dead mahout did not want the animal killed, the tide turned. Phai Phet could live!

Elephants are taunted. Or they are abused physically to the point of being tortured. A bull elephant may be in musth, meaning he is in the mating period of his life. This makes him combative as he looks for a mate. Nothing in his path is safe. A female elephant has its own sensitive periods related to her maternal instincts. Threaten a mother's baby, and a charging elephant toward the threat is almost guaranteed. So when Lek heard about the elephant that killed its mahout, she knew there was an explanation, and that the explanation was most likely something other than a mean or evil animal.

There are still tracts of jungle in and around Baan Lao that no companies will develop because of Noom.

Dennis W. Shepherd

Begging To Die; Begging to Lie

From the time of her mother's death, Lek tried to follow Phong Sri's deathbed mantra—*Stand like a rock!* But standing like a rock really was nothing new to Lek. Her crusade for elephants was never easy. When she disappeared from her university classes to take care of elephants, rumors swirled. Her name was constantly under attack. It was easy to attack a hill tribe student, especially in a college setting where most and perhaps all of her classmates had more money. Lek, the Khamu student, was after all, a second-class citizen.

The rumor around campus was that she had a lover in the mountain jungles. She chose mountaintop rendezvous over science class. Particularly long absences meant just one thing—Lek had gotten pregnant. She escaped the shame by sneaking away from class to have her jungle lover's baby in a crudely built hut deep in the rainforest. In a way, it was a very romantic rumor. It was full of intrigue, nature, raw love, but most important of all—it was totally false!

Rumors based upon ethnic discrimination were embarrassing. But when she entered the public arena of the animal rights activist, she soon found out there were things far worse than mere humiliation. Lek would come face-to-face with hatred so palpable it led to physical pain. Her campaign against "street begging" elephants proved that.

At any given time an estimated two hundred elephants could be found throughout Thailand walking the city streets, each with a mahout bent on exploiting his animal to make a few baht from tourists. Fresh air, jungle foraging spots, rivers for socializing, literally all of the comforts of their natural habitat of these elephants was replaced with the polluted, steel-and-concrete jungle of the city. Preparing such a large animal to stay totally submissive inside a densely populated city with its noises, smells, and people necessarily meant using the most brutal of training methods. It meant beating the elephant senseless.

Typically, a beggar elephant would be taken from block to block as the mahout offered tourists a chance to feed him out of his bag of fruit for a few baht. It didn't take long to wreck the natural diet of the animal. Tourists shoved bananas and other food, sometimes junk food, into the elephant's mouth. Instead of natural foraging, the elephant was kept in a constant state of malnutrition. The tourists had no idea they were contributing to the elephant's downfall. For them, this was a harmless novelty. To some, it was even their way of connecting to nature. To the elephant, it was further separation from its natural environment, being forced to eat on cue.

Sometimes it wasn't the diet that was ruined, but the animal's natural pride. Street-begging elephants were made to do any number of degrading tricks for money. Lek discovered a beggar in her own backyard, begging in Chiang Mai, so she organized a campaign.

After the opening of the elephant park in 1995, becoming fully operational in 1996, Lek began to attract volunteers to help her run the park. Foreign students signed up. This would eventually bring much needed outside attention to Lek's cause. Lek worked out a way for the volunteers to pay their own way, no matter where they were in the world, in return for a place to stay and the opportunity to care for the elephants she rescued. It was an exotic brand of volunteerism. When she embarked on an anti-abuse campaign, her loyal volunteers joined her.

When she found out that a baby elephant was being paraded around in Chiang Mai, she and her band of volunteers took action. This beggar elephant was a real novelty act. He was advertised as a boxing elephant. The mahout dressed up the young elephant in boxing shorts and fitted his front feet with gloves. On cue, the pathetic baby would stand on his hind legs and go through the motions of boxing. It was cruel and demeaning, and Lek planned to put a stop to it.

She followed the mahout from street to street in Chiang Mai. Close by was her tiny foreign army of volunteers holding up signs. One held up a sign in German; another in French; and still another in English. Even though the mahout knew these were protesters, he couldn't get upset at Lek's army because he did not understand what their signs said. Lek held up a sign in Thai. This one he understood: "Don't Support Animal Cruelty!"

It didn't take long for him to see what was happening. People would approach him with baht in hand, take one look at one of the signs, and pull the money back. The mahout stormed over to Lek. She wasn't prepared for what happened next. Even though she tried to shield her face from him with the protest sign, he moved too fast. He sent a vicious fist, punching through her sign and striking Lek squarely in the face. In one crashing instant, she was on the ground, dazed with blood pouring out as if someone had cut her with a knife. Her face was red and her lips swollen. Somehow the hard blow had not only knocked her senseless, she was losing a lot of blood. This was not the era of cell phones and fast responses to emergencies. So, even with the volunteers, it took a long time to get her to the hospital.

At the hospital, the doctor worried about a possible neck injury. Lek was to stay overnight for tests. She had to wear a neck brace. Instead of remaining there, and still in a hospital gown, she ran out, jumped in a *tuk-tuk*, a Thai version of a taxi using a motorcycle, and went home. It was late. Adam was asleep but the television was still on. Her face was still bleeding. She hoped Adam would understand. But when he woke up, he got angry. It was a bad ending for her activism and another sign that her marriage was failing.

All forms of abuse affected Lek's thinking. Each new case and each new type simply strengthened her resolve. Some acts were so cruel, so much more serious than a street-begging elephant that Lek began to think of herself as the elephant defender. Each time she discovered these acts, she thought to herself—"I know you cannot speak. I will speak for you."

Torture during the phaajaan was clearly this kind of abuse. So was the practice of eating elephant meat. Because of the lore connected with elephants, about their long life, their strength, long memory, and high intelligence, some people actually believed that consuming elephant meat gave them special powers. It was when she found out that some in her own family were selling elephant meat from elephants that died at the park that a major rift developed between Lek and these family members.

When one elephant owner asked for her help, she learned of another type of animal cruelty. At the outset all she knew was that an elephant was badly burned. When she arrived in the village, she saw to her own horror that the elephant's face was nearly burned off. She heard the poor animal groaning, obviously suffering terrible pain. It seemed to Lek that all he wanted to do was to die.

She asked the owner how the elephant came to be burned so badly. He told her it happened during a jungle fire. When she asked others, no one knew anything about a fire. When she went to the area, she found nothing to suggest there ever was a fire. The elephant's burns were only to his face. There was no way he could live through such a fire and only suffer facial burns. The owner was lying. As she did in other cases, Lek dug deeper.

What she found was very disturbing. The elephant was a logging elephant. It was a familiar story. He was given very little rest. He became so ill he could barely lift his legs to work. The owner began to beat him to force the work out of him. As he did this, another mahout let out a laugh. When the owner saw his own elephant was making a fool out of him, he decided to punish his elephant in the extreme. He doused the animal's face with a couple gallons of gasoline, and then set fire to him. No case ever stood out as more compelling. Lek had to speak for the elephant.

When Lek learned the full truth, she went to the police. The police laughed at her. They told her it was none of her business. Lek brought her veterinarian friend with her. She hoped to euthanize the suffering giant. Instead of helping her, the police contacted the local newspaper and asked if they were interested in doing a story about an insane lady who thought of elephants as humans.

The story backfired on the police. Instead of falling for the police version, local news reported the incident accurately, that the owner set fire to his own animal. When this news reached the provincial governor, Lek discovered that exposing abuse had serious political consequences. The governor's office issued a denial. The story was wrong. Nothing of the sort ever happens between owners and elephants. This caused one newspaper to send a journalist to the area to investigate. Soon the "elephant burned alive" story, now well documented, was being aired by all of the local media. The officials who thought their version of events would take hold now lost face. Making matters worse, another story was circulating at the same time, one that hurt Lek very badly. The story exposed the elephant meat trade in the country.

Lek found herself opposing governmental forces. The governor told Lek that she had to "make it right." Lek had to issue a statement that the owner had not intentionally burned his elephant. She refused. Noom's teaching took hold once again. "Abandon the truth and you abandon your dignity." Phong Sri's dying words steeled her for the fight: "Stand like a rock!"

Instead of agreeing to a lie, Lek told the provincial governor that both news reports were correct. This man did punish his elephant by burning his entire face. People were consuming elephant meat like it was some magic elixir. A couple of government agents spoke privately with Lek. They reminded her that her ex-husband was a foreigner who needed a valid visa to remain in the country. Despite their differences, Lek always tried to help Adam maintain his visa. But his visa was not the only problem the government men mentioned. They also planned to investigate her tax records to see if there was a problem. Lek asked them what they wanted.

"You know what to do. Call a press conference. Tell them that you lied."

Lek asked for some time to think about their proposal. She called Adam to warn him that unexpected visitors may be asking about his visa. She was confused. On the one hand she could not bring herself to lie. The way the poor elephant was tortured was a fact. That people ate elephant meat was also a fact. On the other hand, terrible things could happen to Adam and to her business.

Adam's advice was simple: "Lek, do what you think is right."

Years of marital turmoil did not change the respect each had for the other. Lek told him that he would be in danger if she told the truth. His stay in Thailand could be cut short. Someone could plant evidence on him and charge him with a crime. But Adam knew Lek too well. He reminded her how stubborn she had always been and he couldn't change that now.

Lek went back to the officials who wanted her to lie to help them save face. They told her that a news conference would be scheduled for the following week. That's when she could make

The Elephant Lady of Thailand

things right. Even before the press event, the same officials began contacting local media, giving them advance word that Lek would confess to her lies. When some of Lek's staunchest supporters heard this, they begged her not to sell out.

Lek went to work. She had seven days to prepare. She assembled photographs and made slides. When the day of the press conference arrived, a large audience awaited. Local news media was joined with international outlets like Reuters and the Associated Press. She put together a solid case. She distributed "proof" envelopes to the media present. Inside were photographs showing the burned-off face of the elephant. Elephant meat she showed was being sold in local markets. Her confession turned out to be a confession of the truth.

Soon after the news conference Thai immigration officials showed up at the travel agent office where Lek and Adam worked. They accused Lek of employing a "westerner" who did not possess the required work visa. Lek asked who sent them. They claimed to be responding to an anonymous call. The only thing Lek could think to do was to threaten to call the news media. When she did, the head of the local immigration office asked her to talk to him first. Nothing came out of this meeting.

More government officials showed up at the travel office, this time when Lek was out of the office. They asked Adam to sit behind the booking counter so they could take pictures. They wanted the pictures to show people that he was working. They would then claim he was working without a visa. They asked one of the office workers to be a witness against him. They demanded to see his passport. Adam told them that Lek kept his passport with her for safekeeping and she could not be reached.

The chief interrogator demanded to use one of the office phones to call his boss. He spent over an hour supposedly making official calls about Adam. When Lek heard about it, she told Adam he could not have been making calls to his office because it was New Year's Day. All government offices were closed. They found out later that the official was calling his friend in southern Thailand.

It was after all of these experiences that Lek's most life-shattering event would occur. She was now a known animal rights activist specializing in exposing abuse to elephants. She stood up to abusers and to those in the Thai government who would try to hide the abuse. Her name was known inside and outside the circles of power. By the fall of 2002, she had already achieved regional success as an elephant advocate. But nothing in her past, from the bout with the boxing elephant owner, to the case of the elephant burned out of pure meanness, would ever eclipse the danger to her work and life as what lay ahead.

Death to the Elephant Lady!

Lek's work to stop the abuse to Thailand's elephants began innocently, when the Golden One walked into her young life. Over the many years that followed, she found ways to translate her passion for these animals into missions that actually helped them. But as sincere as she was in her crusade, she was always careful not to alienate the mahouts and elephant owners who welcomed her help. Even when she discovered the cruel method of trapping wild elephants, and even after she saw firsthand the incredibly painful training method known as the phaajaan, Lek did not burn the bridges she spent so long building. To do so would end her ability to help.

To her, the important question was always how to keep the human masters of hurt elephants satisfied so Lek would be asked back. Part of the answer was to let her evolving Jumbo Express missions work their magic on the entire area each elephant came from. Cure the elephant and help the humans. And part of the answer was to show the owners a better way, a more humane way to train elephants. Lek's method was to educate mahouts, elephant camp owners, and anyone involved in a business requiring trained elephants, whether that business used them for labor or entertainment. She taught them that torture could be replaced with a system of positive reinforcement. Rewards of food, soothing words, and gentle taps could take the place of a torture chamber, jabs with long spears, and deep cuts with sharp knives. "Breaking" an elephant, either its spirit or its bond with its mother, was not necessary.

As brave as Lek was when it came to standing up to those who would abuse the animals, as she did with the man with the boxing baby elephant, she knew that she could not threaten an

The Elephant Lady of Thailand

entire industry without serious consequences. She could be blackballed from working with elephants. Word would spread that she was no longer welcome. When that word spread to the villages, there would be no more Jumbo Express missions. There were other possible consequences. She knew of cases where the competition between elephant camps led to the most extreme consequences, where people were shot or burned. So her campaign to ban torture was a measured one, starting at the grass roots, teaching villagers and mahouts that it was not necessary.

During one of her trips into the jungle, Lek shot video footage of a village training elephants. In fact, it was footage of the phaajaan. From time to time, she would show it to close friends so they could understand the horror behind this practice. One such friend was an American who became a supporter of Lek's work in 1996. She helped raise money to help Lek fight against elephant abuse. She accompanied Lek into the jungle so she could witness the torture that elephants suffered for the sake of elephant camp owners. She saw firsthand the phaajaan being practiced.

Lek trusted her not to reveal the secrets of the villagers they visited. Like a journalist protects sources, Lek was careful not to do anything that would interrupt her access to villages that needed her help in curing sick and injured elephants. "Amy"[3] seemed to understand this. Lek trusted her more and more. She became one of her closest friends. In the fall of 2002, Amy asked for a copy of the phaajaan video. Lek gave her one.

On October 18, 2002, a well-known international animal rights organization released startling video footage to the public. PETA, or People for the Ethical Treatment of Animals, added to their list of unethical animal practices the torture of elephants. They released video of the phaajaan. It was the same video Lek had made. It was the video she had given to Amy. Now the world would see what Lek was campaigning against. Confidences between Lek and Amy were compromised. Confidences between Lek and the villagers were compromised. Lek's entire life's work was now in jeopardy, because not only

---

[3] Amy is not the friend's real name.

did PETA release the tape to the public, it called for a boycott of Thailand's entire tourism industry.

In one day Sangduen Lek Chailert went from a local Chiang Mai heroine, the famous elephant lady, to one of the most hated women in Thailand. The entire country was cast in a negative light through the prism of the phaajaan video footage, and Lek was the cause. Initial reaction came in the form of dozens upon dozens of angry phone calls to Lek's Chiang Mai office. The calls came mainly from tourist agencies that relied on doing business in northern Thailand, in and around Chiang Mai.

Just one day after PETA's release, Thai companies including the elephant camps, made a startling public announcement: Phaajaan does not exist in Thailand! The video footage released by PETA must be a fake. Either that or it was filmed outside of Thai borders, perhaps in Burma.

Lek reeled over this announcement. She knew what the truth was because *she shot the film*. Thai TV Channel 9 arranged an interview with her. She was asked about the claim that the video footage originated outside of Thailand. She did the only thing she could do; she told the truth. She told her interviewer that she shot the video in a Thai village. Nothing took place outside of the country. If PETA's release of the tape was a bombshell, Lek's statement, essentially calling an entire industry a liar, was all-out war. It was war declared upon everyone and everything that wanted to defend against a charge that they were abusing the national symbol. A powerful group of interested parties emerged. This coalition included key members and agencies of the Thai government itself.

Almost as soon as Lek spoke to the television cameras, the target changed. She took ownership of the video. She vouched for the fact that this was a Thai village. She became the subject of public ridicule and vicious attacks by several sources. Thai TV Channel 5 accused her of doctoring the video, of making it up. Once the focus shifted to Lek, nothing was off-limits when it came to vilifying her.

Her marriage to Adam was used against her. Obviously she was not a loyal Thai because she had married a foreigner! Her hill tribe family was also attacked. Some claimed that one of her brothers was a merchant who illegally sold wood from timber that was banned for commercial use. The attacks mounted. Lek could not believe what a devastating disaster the release of a few minutes of video caused. One media outlet went so far as to associate her with a known drug dealer, claiming her name, Chailert, was similar to the drug dealer's and that she was related.

The national scandal produced odd alliances. Elephant camps seemed to be joined in the attacks against Lek by animal rights groups. Thai conservationists felt betrayed by Lek. She let PETA have all the credit when this was a great revelation discovered by a Thai citizen. Obviously Lek sold out to PETA, when she and Thailand should have been in the forefront of exposing the awful practice of phaajaan, not PETA. In an amazing display of unity among the strangest of bedfellows, Lek watched as she was soundly condemned by the Thai news media, elephant camp owners, tourist industry representatives, and animal rights groups.

Two days after her interview on Channel 9, someone threw a large rock at her office window in Chiang Mai, shattering the glass. Passersby shouted insults like, "Your boss is a bitch!" More angry phone calls poured in. Another press conference was held, this time by the Department of Forestry and Thai Police. They issued an ominous announcement. An investigation was underway to see if Lek broke any laws. If she did, she would be arrested!

On October 28, 2002, the Tourist Authority for the Northern Region of Thailand provided an outlet for the elephant camp owners to make public statements regarding the allegations by PETA. This included over twenty camp owners from the Chiang Mai area, and over forty total. In fact, meeting at this press conference were most of the elephant camp owners of northern Thailand, representatives from elephant rights groups thought to be sympathetic with Lek's work, Thai military, and the son of the Karen owner of the elephant in the phaajaan footage. The media event had one purpose in mind: to prove that the video evidence of the phaajaan was false.

The authorities gave the microphone to an eyewitness, a young Karen man who claimed to watch the entire phaajaan as

Lek filmed it. He said that a woman named Lek put the villagers up to creating this footage. She staged it to look like elephant abuse. The blood on the elephant seen in the video was in fact fake, nothing more than red sauce like ketchup. Lek and some unidentified westerners paid the villagers to act as if they were beating the elephants. The son of the village leader confirmed this account.

Brought before the cameras was the Karen tribe owner of the elephant seen stabbed and tortured in the video. He now claimed that it was Lek who told the phaajaan participants to stab the elephant! Someone at the news conference made a chilling comment: In the old days there was a simple solution to liars like Lek. They would have their throats cut!

On October 31, Karen villagers were summoned to the Chiang Mai district office under the guise of getting electricity for their villages. The real reason was to testify against Lek. They were instructed to say that she stole elephants. Fliers were distributed throughout the villages warning the people about Lek. She was not an elephant savior at all. Even her humanitarian efforts for the poor jungle villages were undermined. She wasn't really taking them much needed supplies and medicines. No, she was a lackey of U.S. drug companies taking experimental drugs to poor villagers to see if they worked. Things were spinning out of control!

Lek was appalled by the barrage of attacks. Not only was she scorned and a national disgrace, but her life was at stake. The lives of those around her—her family, friends, and employees—they were all in danger! Her years of building rapport with villages and elephant owners seemed to be erased in just a few days of baseless attacks. Powerful groups united against her. The release of the phaajaan video to the world meant Lek couldn't walk the streets of Chiang Mai in safety. The entire episode was destroying Lek's work and threatened to destroy Lek too. Rumors swirled. One in particular began to circulate. Lek heard it from friends. She heard it from anonymous calls to her office. She would be kidnapped and never heard from again. Lek must die. She was too dangerous for Thailand!

Back to Happier Times: The Story of Gingmai

Eight months before PETA released the phaajaan video and Lek's life was forever changed, something quite different happened to Lek. Still in the doldrums over Phong Sri's premature passing, Lek received a jolt of happiness that brought her back to the living. In a very special and unusual way, Lek became a mother. The story of her motherhood would itself become entangled in the disastrous PETA episode. But in the beginning at least, only happiness fell on Lek Chailert.

Of all the elephant rescues that Lek made, from the days when they were merely "rucksack" missions, to the carefully planned trips known as Jumbo Expresses, of them all there is one that stands out as the most memorable rescue she ever conducted. That's because it resulted in the most beloved elephant of her life. If the Golden One was the most important elephant of her childhood, Gingmai[4] was the most important elephant in her entire life.

Gingmai was just a few days old when Lek first saw him in December of 2001. Shortly after his mother gave birth to him, she was killed. She was shot in a cornfield in Karen territory. When the first Karen villagers saw the dead mother, they assumed her baby had been stillborn. But he was not. The shocked baby, new to the world outside of his mother's womb, fled into the jungle. He wandered through the jungle rainforest hopelessly lost. Everything frightened him. There was no one to comfort him. He fled in a panic. Trees looked like giant beasts. The ground was filled with a million new threats, smaller creatures than the tree beasts, but things that crawled and stung. He darted through the underbrush. When something spooked him, he would charge ahead full speed. It was after one of his "fright runs" that he got himself wedged between two small trees. He remained there in agony for three days and three nights.

---

[4] The story of Gingmai described here is based upon interviews with Lek and upon her own account published in two separate articles appearing in the local publication, *Good Morning Chiangmai*, in its April and May, 2006 editions.

At night, Karen villagers heard Gingmai's high-pitched baby moans of pain. Because ghost lore abounds in Thailand, especially among the hill tribe people, the Karen villagers mistook his cries in the night for the ghost of Gingmai's mother, come back to haunt them. For three nights the village was under the spell of the crying elephant ghost. On the fourth day, village boys overcame their fear and decided to track down the source of the moans. That's when they found Gingmai, stuck between trees. He was bleeding and in great pain. He hadn't eaten and was still suffering from the severe shock of losing his mother.

The boys' first efforts to free him, by pulling and pushing him, were unsuccessful. The more they tried, the more Gingmai screamed in agony, and contorted his baby elephant body, making things worse. He screamed every time his baby skin rubbed against the tree bark. It soon became clear to his rescuers that the only way to free him was to cut him out of his trap by cutting the trees that bound him. That's what the young boys did. They cut him out with a saw. As soon as he was free, he collapsed to the ground.

The boys brought water to him from a nearby river. They used a long, hollowed out bamboo stalk as a straw. The suffering newborn sucked it in as fast as they could supply it. When the villagers realized there was no ghost, they had a very sick baby on their hands. No one knew how to cure Gingmai. They decided to call in an elephant expert. They contacted Lek.

To save Gingmai, Lek had to become a mother substitute. She had to find a way to show him that love did not die with his elephant mother. Lek had never tried this before. She attended the births of elephants, acting as an elephant's midwife, but to take on the role of mother was something very different. Her sister, Sakorn, owned a pig farm with her husband. They agreed to let Gingmai stay there to recuperate. Lek took the sick baby there and built a pen for him.

It did not look promising. Three days of fighting to free himself from the trees left deep cuts all over his body. The wounds had become infected. The baby had an awful smell from all of the puss that filled his many wounds. He was also badly sunburned making his skin all the more sensitive. He could not stand on his own feet. He was too weak. His struggle with the trees left deep cuts on both hips, some reaching all the way to the bone. Nothing about him looked normal. The water may have helped him, but it could not cure the infection spreading through his body. And nothing, not food and not water, could erase the mental scar that losing his mother had left. He may not have wanted to stand or to live for that matter.

Lek decided the only hope was to force-feed him the nutrients his body craved. After quickly constructing a mattress for him, she turned her attention to feeding him. She bought baby milk formula and began feeding him warm milk as soon as she could. Gingmai gulped down three gallons in no time. Almost immediately Gingmai developed diarrhea, forcing Lek to adjust his "baby formula."

Next, the little doctor of Baan Lao took over to cure the infections. She spent the next several days dressing his wounds and feeding him. She cleaned the cuts and applied an herbal medicine to keep bugs from entering them. December can be very cold in the hills and mountains of northern Thailand, so Lek built a fire each morning to warm the baby elephant.

She named the orphan Gingmai. In Thai this means "tree branch." Lek wanted him to have a name that invoked the jungle spirit that saved him. The two trees were located perilously close to a precipice. Had he not gotten stuck between the two young trees, he would have stepped off a high cliff, into a deep chasm, to certain death. The spirit of the jungle, in this case embodied by the trees, helped him survive. Men killed his mother, but nature saved the baby.

Despite his traumatic entry into this world, Gingmai was a beautifully formed baby. His features were perfect. Long black hair sprouted above his eyes, gradually turning brown around his ears. His tongue was a beautiful pink. His baby trunk was beautiful. There was nothing particularly pretty about his eyes except that they were dark and penetrating. They had the worried look of someone who had suffered too much already.

Had he stayed in his elephant family, someone would have taken over the job of raising him. It's not uncommon for an auntie to take over the job of mothering an orphan, even one from another herd. But Gingmai had no such luck. His mother died suddenly and any chance that he would be adopted ended with his flight into the jungle. In fact, Lek suspected that his mother's family disowned him once they saw she was dead. That may be the reason Gingmai fled alone into the dark. He was a motherless child that the others had turned against. No one wanted him—until Lek found him!

Lek bought powdered milk in bulk from a local store. She mixed it as carefully as any mother would mix her child's baby formula and then warmed it. She fed Gingmai from a bottle. She even found a way to burp him, gently massaging his stomach. When he slept, she stayed with him so he would not wake up alone. She was afraid he would have flashbacks to when he was trapped in the jungle. Sometimes she fell asleep only to be awoken by Gingmai's soft feet rubbing against her face.

During his recuperation period, Lek never left him except for very short periods. He was especially nervous in his small pen. Lek stayed close to him when he seemed to be remembering the horrible way he came into this life. She would hold him, or pet him so that for each frightful look he gave, a comforting touch would stave off his fear. Noises especially frightened him. When a dog barked or a rooster crowed, Lek was always close to Gingmai. Gingmai grew dependent on her. If he wanted to wake her, he would push her gently with his trunk or feet until she got up. Then he would lick her nose with his tongue. In all his bodily communication with Lek, he was telling her he loved her and needed her.

Lek spent many weeks taking care of his wounds. After four weeks, the wounds began to markedly improve. After six weeks, she took him for his first trip beyond his elephant pen. While many others who saw him gave him very little hope of surviving, Lek's constant care and love seemed to heal not only his battered little body, but his broken heart. Gingmai began to look like a very healthy baby elephant. The pinkish hue of his trunk turned darker. He had overcome the sunburn. He was past the skin scraped raw during his jungle imprisonment. Long eyelashes formed. Physically, he was almost back to being a healthy baby elephant.

One night Lek decided she needed a break from what was sometimes an around-the-clock watch over Gingmai. She pitched a tent a few hundred yards away from him so she could have one decent night's sleep. She had gotten thoroughly rundown from the daily routine of nursing Gingmai. It was a beautiful night. The full moon was shining almost as brightly as the sun. She slept deeply knowing that Gingmai was safely behind a locked gate.

Lek suddenly woke from her sound sleep, to the sounds of a rustling noise outside her tent. When she opened her eyes, a beautiful shadow danced on the canvas above her. It was Gingmai. She could see him trying to push his tongue through her tent. He had followed her scent. Lek knew the two were inseparable now. She saved his life and even found a way to replace the love that was destroyed when his mother was killed.

It was clear that the elephant knew how to unlatch the gate of his shelter. Lek still needed to rest, so she told her volunteer to make a stronger latch. The next night she moved her tent even farther from Gingmai's shelter. A volunteer worker stayed with the elephant. Early the next morning she heard the volunteer yelling, "Oh, no!" Soon after that Gingmai barreled into her tent. He would not be denied.

Gingmai would only take milk from Lek or from someone with a piece of clothing with Lek's scent. When Lek fed him, he liked to wrap his trunk around her neck and drink through his mouth. He loved his substitute mom very much.

By the fall of 2002, Gingmai's health was much better. As he improved, Lek took on another orphan, another baby elephant whose mother burned to death. The new orphan she named Hope. Soon after that, a third baby named Jabu joined the other two. Now Lek's life was filled with love. Virtually every waking hour was spent caring for the three babies.

The only comfort room facility on the farm was an outhouse. She couldn't even go to the bathroom without three babies standing guard and sometimes trying to muscle their way inside. But all of the motherly attention Lek gave them paid off. The three elephants were eating together, taking mud baths together, and napping together. When they slept, Lek had to be there to comfort them, like a mother comforts her child at bedtime.

There were accidents. Hope was much more difficult to "tame" and bring around than Gingmai. Like Gingmai, he came into the world witnessing the death of his mother, not shot like

Gingmai's, but burned to death. He became just as frightened and mistrustful of people as Gingmai. Lek spent a lot of her time trying to gain his confidence. One day Hope was playing with Lek and very innocently jammed his head into her chest. He was over four hundred pounds at the time and had baby elephant tusks already. He cracked a couple of her ribs.

When she could, Lek took the babies to the jungle to let them roam at will. During one of these "freedom" walks, Hope and Gingmai disappeared, obviously enjoying their unrestricted state. Not long afterwards, Lek heard Hope screaming. She ran to him only to discover that he had stuck his trunk into a bees' nest. Lek spent the next several minutes fighting off the bees that were stinging Hope. She got Hope safely away, but only after bee stings covered her own body.

One day Gingmai and his new best friend, Hope, were missing again. Volunteers spent several hours looking for them. Could they have run back into the jungle and returned to nature for real? Did someone put a mahout up to stealing them so they could become street-begging elephants? In fact, the two babies had run to a large patch of mud where they lounged together until their entire bodies were caked with mud. They doubled back to the tents, slipping inside one of the larger ones erected for volunteer workers. When the volunteers found them, they were both lying where the beds used to stand, crushing them, soundly asleep with covers pulled over their eyes. It was an amazing and beautiful sight.

Taking care of these three elephants meant that Lek had no other life. She could not socialize with the human animals out there. Going out with friends was out of the question. Making time for herself was impossible. The baby elephants took up all of her time. Raising three elephants was for the elephant lady just like having her own children. She did not mind giving up her privacy for them. It was one of the happiest times of her life.

The Elephant Lady of Thailand

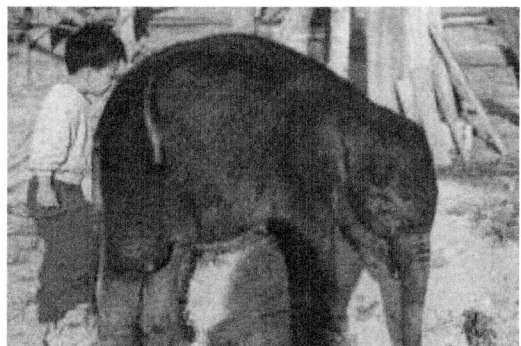

Lek's beloved Gingmai. Photo from Animalfair, an organization supporting animal rescue and fairness.

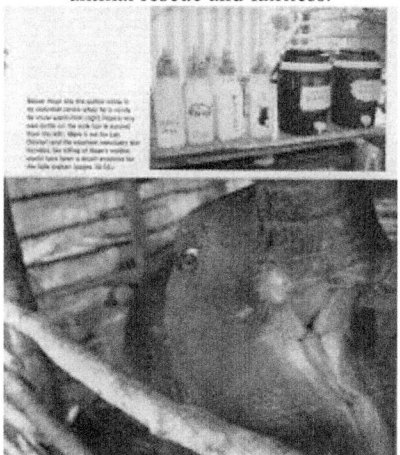

By the fall of 2002, Gingmai's health was much better. As he improved, Lek took on another orphan, another baby elephant whose mother burned to death. The new orphan she named Hope.

The Worst of Times: Lek in Exile

It was shortly after this beautiful time in her life that PETA released the phaajaan video and Lek found herself not fighting for the lives of her baby elephants, but for her own survival. Her life to be sure was filled with ups and downs, but the extremes seemed to rule her life. Phong Sri died. Her marriage fell apart. Her hill tribe family itself seemed to come apart as her dream for an elephant nature park turned into one large family argument. After such a dark period, three beautiful babies miraculously appeared, giving Lek a new lease on her life and her dreams.

This was followed by her darkest days yet, as the entire country seemed to scorn her as a traitor.

When her world turned upside down, a lot of people were out to get her. Where the threats came from was not always clear. It was easy to say the government was not happy with her, but what government? Who is the government? It was obvious that elephant camps, especially the "mafia" camps targeted Lek. But which ones sent agents after her? If she could not name names, she could not accuse the government, people in the government, or camps owned by those who wanted her dead. But one thing Lek knew with certainty. There was a shadow force of men out to stop her. She could not identify anyone in particular, but she could feel the danger!

Government agencies began to line up against Lek. Some called on the government to kick her out of the country. Media outlets made a plea to Lek to stand up and apologize for the great insult she caused to her country. Lek refused. She hadn't done anything wrong.

One of Lek's oldest and closest friends turned on her. Lek saw her in a local shop with her son and daughter. When one of her children recognized "Auntie Lek," the long-time best friend pulled her children back and told them to stay away from Lek. When Lek asked her to explain, she told her that Lek was now an enemy of the people. If she was seen with her, she could lose her job. Lek was stunned by the betrayal.

Another friend tried to trick Lek into admitting she lied about the PETA tape. "How much did they pay you? I heard PETA gave you sixty million baht for the video. Is that true?"

Someone put her friend up to spying on Lek. She was trying to get her to incriminate herself, but she wasn't a very good informant. Lek saw through it. She wanted to know who Lek's friend was, the one who originally received the phaajaan video footage. Lek pretended to have forgotten. After this encounter, Lek avoided this "friend" altogether. Later, this same person called to apologize. Her boss ordered her to go to the village where the video was shot and try to prove that Lek was a liar. When she did, all she learned was that Lek was telling the truth all along. Now she was ashamed and called Lek to ask for forgiveness. She also called to warn her that she must leave. Lek needed to run away soon before the killer or kidnapper arrived.

Rumors grew and spread. When she went to the local market to buy bananas in bulk for her elephants, the market vendor refused to sell to her. "You have over 200 million from your friends. You insulted the country. We won't sell to you any more."

Local newspapers ran stories citing exorbitant figures of money paid to Lek. There was literally no place she could hide in Chiang Mai without someone knowing who she was and believing she was the enemy of the nation.

The government went so far as to track down the shaman in charge of the phaajaan that was at the center of the controversy. Members of the Thai military tried to persuade him to admit that Lek set the whole thing up. Instead, what they found was a man like Noom. He could not lie. Shamans believe that when you lie about elephants, elephants will kill you. This shaman told the authorities exactly what they did not want to hear. He told the truth. He explained that he had been around the phaajaan ritual from the time he was a teenager. He was in his nineties when they questioned him. He also said that Lek's only reason for being in his village at the time the video was shot was as an observer.

The government men tried to shake his faith in Lek. They told him that Lek was paid millions. Didn't she offer him part of this? If she didn't, then she cheated him. The shaman was an honorable man. He did not fall for the lies. He would not change his story. They tried to scare him, claiming that PETA was trying to have him arrested. The old man did not budge. Even at the prospect of going to jail, he held fast to the truth.

The shaman's son was not of the same mind. He called Lek and accused her of causing trouble for his father in the name of making millions. The son believed the authorities.

The shaman's interrogators were relentless in trying to get him to admit that Lek paid him to stage the phaajaan. The best they could get was the not so startling admission that Lek brought his family fish and some eggs when she visited. Local media exploited even this with headlines suggesting that she obtained her phaajaan video at an extremely inexpensive price, for just ten eggs and some salted fish!

The pressure on Lek and her family continued to build. Government men went to see Lek's father. He made an ambiguous apology for "whatever" his daughter had done.

Lek heard that an arrest warrant had been issued against her. She decided that her only safe course was to go underground. She would flee the familiar surroundings of Chiang Mai, her home when she was not in the jungle taking care of elephants.

It was the darkest of times. The way the entire country turned on Lek was devastating. Close friends were lost. Office staff doubted her. Members of her family turned against her. One of the leading newspapers in Thailand, the *Bangkok Post*, printed many wild accusations against her.

There was just one person in all of Thailand who Lek could turn to for help. She was a member of the royal family, a distant relative of the king. Princess Rangsrinopadorn Yukol was, like Lek, a protector of Thailand's elephant population. A dedicated animal and forestry conservationist, she formed a special bond with Lek and her fight to save elephants.

When the princess saw what was happening to her friend, she called Lek with an urgent warning. She told Lek that her life was very much in danger. She invited her to Bangkok to stay at the palace. It seemed the only safe place in Thailand. Lek was now officially on the run. From her friends, including one royal princess, the advice was the same. Run or die.

Before she left, she met with her brother, Boonta. He had the same warning as the others. She was in grave danger. Lek told him defiantly, "I'll leave now, but someday I will return victorious."

At the end of October 2002, Lek fled to Bangkok temporarily to the safety of the princess's palace. It was an uneasy arrangement. The princess staunchly defended Lek to the press, but when that same press learned of Lek's location, they turned to pursuing the princess. Lek did not want this for her special protector.

While in the capital city another very special person asked to see Lek. She was a member of the Thai parliament, a senator.

Lek agreed, but, ever wary, she would not agree to a meeting place until minutes before the scheduled meeting.

When the two met, the legislator told Lek that she wanted to help her. Lek was relieved. Finally, she found someone outside of her own small circle of friends whom she could trust. Lek opened up to the woman. She told her about her trips into the jungle, helping abused and otherwise injured elephants in Thailand and in Burma. She poured her heart out. She really wanted to win this important member of parliament to her side. She told her the truth about elephant training in and around Thailand. She told her about the elephant trap. When she was finished, the woman thanked Lek profusely. She even asked her to work with her on special programs for elephants.

Not long after their meeting, newspaper articles appeared that suggested that Lek made several illegal border crossings. Still others implicated her in the drug trade. The interview with the senator was just another trap. The senator took the information Lek gave her during their meeting and turned it against Lek.

When Lek was linked to such dangerous elements as drug dealers, her life was in grave danger. Snuffing her out would do the country a favor. Reckless stories about her were printed, copied by others, and reprinted. One report said that her own father turned his back on her, calling her the black sheep of the family. Her father, Sa-Nguan, and Lek had their differences, but he never resorted to calling her names or joining in with others who regarded her as a traitor. What he actually said was that Lek was unique. She was so different from his other children. She was a vegetarian. She prized her work with animals. But the story was picked up and distributed all over Thailand that Lek's own father had called her an outcast.

With so many crazy and dangerous forces swirling around her, trying to incriminate her, trying to arrest her, and maybe trying to kill her, Lek gave up her refuge in the palace. She told the princess that she did not want to bring disgrace to her. She continued her underground journey with a couple of close friends, still trying to remain invisible to the rest of the world.

She did not have much money. With the help of the princess and friends, she was able to retain an attorney. Her friends—real friends who believed in Lek and in her work—sent money that would prove crucial in keeping her safe from the public view. Even Amy, the woman she trusted with the phaajaan video, tried to help Lek. It was a strange army of supporters, led by a princess, peopled by foreigners, and included the very person who sparked the entire episode with PETA.

Lek's underground existence was dismal. She was forced to flee into the largest city, Bangkok, over three hundred and fifty miles away from Chiang Mai. At least there she was just one in over eleven million faces. She lived in constant fear, waiting to see if a stranger might pull a gun or knife on her as she walked the city streets. She worried about being forced into a car and never being heard from again. She changed her living quarters often, moving from one cheap hotel or student hostel to another. She lived in some of the seediest sections of Bangkok including the Patpong District. Known for its nightlife, and once the heart of the city's sex trade, Lek spent days and nights there to avoid being detected. She even resorted to a disguise to ensure that no one, not even in Patpong, would recognize her as the elephant lady accused of selling out the nation.

One evening her friends took her to a strip joint filled with prostitutes. When she asked why they brought her to such a place, they told her to just sit and watch. What she saw were strippers and customers trying to strike sex deals. One of her friends told her to look for the police. There were police coming and going all the time. No one was arrested. No matter how blatant the propositions were, nobody was arrested. "That's reality, Lek," said one of her friends. "People break the law right under their noses and nothing happens."

It may have been a stark lesson in the real world of Bangkok nightlife, but it did not change anything. She was still trapped, trapped by her own upbringing, trapped into being honest. When the whole world seemed bent on moving her away from her true character, she refused to change. After her Patpong "lesson," she moved from place to place, flophouse to flophouse, more often. Sometimes she would hear threatening whispers.

"Do you think it's her?" one store clerk would say to another.

The Elephant Lady of Thailand

"No, I don't think so." If they recognized her name in the hotel registry, she was told to leave.

"We don't want you here."

As Lek moved from place to place, there were changing stories about her in the media. Sometimes she was reported to be kidnapped. Sometimes she was dead! The lies about Lek actually harming elephants instead of helping them continued. At one point a television talk show broadcast new lies and put a telephone number on the screen with this message: "Lek Chailert, if you are out there, call this number and respond to the charges."

When she saw this she was on the edge of a breakdown. She picked up the phone to dial the number on the screen. She wanted to confront her accusers. Instead she called her attorney. He told her not to respond. It was all a trap to find her or trick her into saying something she shouldn't. She didn't call. Instead, she went into the bathroom, turned the shower on, and screamed out her anger.

Many people were searching for Lek. The unscrupulous would stop at nothing to find her. Whether it was to get a big news scoop, or to harm her, someone was always on her trail. Some men even went so far as to scare an innocent child to try to find her. They went up to Lek's eight-year-old niece and lied to her. They told her there were other people, really bad people who wanted to cut her aunt's throat. The little girl was petrified. The men told her if she would just tell them where Lek was they could help her. When they left, Lek's niece was shaking in fear.

On the run, Lek became a ghost of her old self. She lost weight. She tried to eat, but being in a state of constant worry left her stomach tied up in knots. More and more her eyes resembled the eyes of the abused elephants she encountered, like Pang Boon Ma's—eyes without a soul. They were so used to feeling nothing but pain, so Lek stared out at the world with a ghostly, unfeeling stare.

Losing her taste for food was only one effect the pressure was having on her. She was growing increasingly paranoid. Phone calls were just ways for her enemies to find her. Friends were really spies. Her family could not be trusted. No one could be trusted. She wondered about her lawyer. The truth was upside down. The whole nation seemed to believe the lies. Maybe the lies were the truth and she was wrong. There was no dividing line between the truth and something else. It was all a bad dream! Lek was losing more than her taste; she was losing her mind!

Lek's Personal Phaajaan: Breaking Her Love

In one short month after the October news conference that sent her fleeing from Chiang Mai, Lek seemed to lose everything. But despite the daily fear and personal degradation she was made to feel, she could always draw strength from her work. All the lies in the country could not take away her good deeds with the elephant population of Thailand. And the mounting threats from the elephant camp cartels could not destroy the beautiful love she had for Gingmai and her other two baby orphans, Jabu and Hope. The babies were her only comfort as she hid from public view.

During her first weeks living in the underground, a letter made its way to Lek. A group of people wanted to meet with her. It was a very ominous letter. The letter did not identify who she was to meet with. Either Lek would follow instructions, meeting at the designated time and place, or someone close to Lek would be hurt or killed.

She knew if she ever agreed to such a meeting, she would be kidnapped and killed. She knew what rival camp owners did to each other. Men and women were shot. They were left to burn in their cars. She saw firsthand how a wealthy man like Mr. N. could be shot to pieces by the mafia camp forces. Her friends knew Lek was on the run. They also knew that they were at risk just by knowing her. So by not going to the meeting, Lek was not changing the status quo. Lek ignored the threat.

Even as she hid from public view, she had to take care of her elephants. While in Bangkok, she arranged for milk purchases shipped in bulk from overseas. When she received the threatening letter, Lek was in the process of arranging for nearly a half ton of milk to be shipped from Bangkok to Chiang Mai. It was being flown into Bangkok from abroad. She went to the Bangkok airport to sign for it and pick it up.

The Elephant Lady of Thailand

When she got there, an airport official recognized her. A bureaucratic nightmare followed. First, she had to pay 25,000 baht in customs fees. Then she was sent from office to office. From the customs office she was sent to the agriculture section. Once there, she was again sent away, this time to the food and drug section.

The customs office threatened to fine her nine hundred baht per day for each day the milk remained in Bangkok. So Lek arranged with a shipping company to ship it to Chiang Mai. That was another four thousand baht. She was determined to get that milk for her elephants. As each new charge came up, she had to find the money by going to friends.

The milk was finally sent to Chiang Mai. She sent someone to pick it up. A new bill was waiting, this time for three thousand baht. Once again she arranged payment; once again she was told she could not have the milk. The food and drug office had not approved its release. Lek gave up. Everyone in the bureaucratic chain had been alerted to make things impossible for Lek.

Harassment continued on other fronts. The pig farm where the babies recuperated was also under attack. Government agents investigated her brother-in-law, Sakorn's husband, who owned the pig farm where Gingmai was raised. They challenged him to show he had clear title to his house. The foreign volunteers who helped Lek with her elephants were suddenly asked to turn in their passports for a special review.

It was too much for Lek. Hiding was no good. Even if the suspected assassins could not find her, there were other forces bent on hurting those she cared about. She decided she must end her exile, if only long enough to take care of her orphans and reassure her friends that she was not giving up the fight to clear her name. She returned to Chiang Mai.

Before she became an outlaw, Lek could reach large segments of the public about her work. Her ability to spread the word about elephants put her well ahead of other animal conservationists in Chiang Mai and in Thailand. Her campaign against street-begging elephants was very real, and she had the bruises to prove it. One day she sat down and wrote a fictional account of this abuse in her illustrated book, *Boon the Street-Walking Elephant*. To teach people how unbounded love can save an orphan baby elephant, she arranged a television documentary about her work with Gingmai. It aired while she was on the run. It was called: "Love Can Heal." Meanness, torture, pain: none of that was necessary. More people learned about her orphan elephants. No one could doubt that Gingmai was her special one.

On November 26, 2002, she awoke to a dream. But it was not a dream. She was finally back at her sister's farm, back with baby Gingmai. It was a beautiful day. No more was she living in flophouses. Patpong was just a bad memory. She was home, or at least at her sister's home. She was back to take care of her three orphans. She took Gingmai for a morning walk. After all she had been through, just spending a few hours alone with him was a wonderful thing. She was so happy with her baby, now a very healthy little elephant.

Both Lek and Gingmai had been through a torture chamber, a type of phaajaan, in which their love of life was severely tested. But both were still alive, and, despite all of Lek's recent troubles, they were still together. Both had survived their separate ordeals, although Lek now seemed to be in a much more precarious situation than Gingmai. When they returned from the walk, Lek put Gingmai in his shelter and went into town to buy food.

Before she left, something strange happened. Gingmai fought with her. He was extremely upset, sensing that she was leaving him. She did the best she could to calm him. It was just like the early days of raising Gingmai, when Lek had to help him overcome his mistrust of people. But Gingmai didn't want her to go. Lek hugged him. Gingmai gave her a hug back with his trunk, but when he did he pulled off her necklace. Phong Sri had given the necklace to her daughter. Gently, Lek asked Gingmai to give it back. Obediently, almost like a child who knows he's done something wrong, Gingmai opened his trunk and dropped the necklace into her hands.

Lek left the orphans in the care of two volunteers and a couple of employees. Then she went to a local supermarket for supplies. The volunteers were sound asleep when Lek left for the store. They had been up all night caring for the elephants, making milk formula.

The Elephant Lady of Thailand

Two men appeared at the farm. They asked one of the farm employees where the elephants were kept. They specifically wanted to see Gingmai. They said that they were veterinarians from the Agriculture Department. They wanted to examine Gingmai to see if he needed to be vaccinated. While one of these men kept up a conversation with the employee, the other went to Gingmai's shelter. It was a short visit and the men left.

Minutes after they left the pig farm, Gingmai began to change. He walked in circles and fidgeted constantly, unable to control himself. He banged his head against the fence over and over again. He gagged uncontrollably as if trying to vomit. His eyes turned from a beautiful ebony to a ghoulish red.

One of the employees saw the changes and called Lek. She was at the checkout counter about to pay for her purchases. As she listened to the symptoms, she stood there puzzled over the sudden change. She thought back to the food she fed him in the morning. Nothing she fed him could make him that sick.

As she talked with her employee on her cell phone, she heard about the visit of the two men. They were there to check on Gingmai's vaccination, but that didn't make sense to Lek. He was too young for any vaccination. When she heard that one man went to see Gingmai, and the other one kept her employee busy, Lek suspected the worst.

"What kind of car were they driving?" she asked, now in a panic. "Was there a government seal on the door?"

The two men parked too far away from the farm to be able to identify the car. The employee did remember that one of the men wore a uniform. That's when it hit her. That's when it all became clear to Lek. These men were sent there to kill her baby, to kill Gingmai. Lek bolted out of the market. She left all of her purchases on the counter. She had to get back to the farm and save Gingmai. The men poisoned him. The letter she received threatening those around her had come true. But they weren't trying to kill her family. They were trying to kill something just as precious in Gingmai.

When she arrived at the shelter, she saw exactly what was described to her over the phone minutes earlier. Gingmai was banging his head against the shelter. His eyes were blood red. He stared out at her like a mad bull about to charge. He seemed to be somewhere else, in another world. He was no longer her baby. He couldn't keep his balance. He no longer recognized Lek.

When she opened his pen, he ran out of the shelter. He ran like a crazed animal intent on getting to water. There was a pond nearby familiar to the babies. When he reached the pond, he sucked the water into his body in a desperate effort to stop the poison from killing him. He was on fire inside and this was his only way of drowning the flames. He squirmed in agony beneath a barbed wire fence. He was screaming wildly, his death shriek piercing Lek's ears and heart.

Suddenly, he came back to her. He found her. Somehow through all the pain, and once lost to the insanity caused by the poison, Gingmai found his human mother again. She was as confused and dazed as her baby. What she saw was horrifying. Blood was oozing out of Gingmai. It was coming out of every orifice. Blood dripped from his mouth and even his eyes—more seeped out of his anal opening. More still came from his trunk. Whatever the evil assassins had given him, it was destroying his body and brain.

Through the confusion and pain, Gingmai managed a short moment of recognition. He found Lek's neck with his trunk. Still screaming in agony, he gently wrapped it around her, giving her one final touch, one last remembrance of his love for her.

Lek cried for help. She begged for someone to call the vet. She held her phone in her hand in a hopeless gesture, trying to find one last lifeline to help. It was too late. She held Gingmai tightly, listening to his last screams of pain. Gingmai held Lek, the only one he ever trusted. She was his substitute mother. The poison coursed through his body, destroying his insides. Gingmai died in Lek's arms.

Others from the farm surrounded Lek and Gingmai. The orphan's trunk went limp. Someone said, "He's dead." Lek threw her cell phone away. Everyone was crying. Lek was crying and screaming uncontrollably. She once told a friend that if anything ever happened to Gingmai, she didn't know if she could go on. Now he was dead and she felt hopeless. All she could do was wail in grief and anger. Several minutes later someone pulled her away from Gingmai.

Hope and Jabu were petrified by all of the commotion. They heard everything. They heard their baby brother go insane with pain. They heard Lek's screams. When they could not take it anymore, the two orphans ran to a tree and just stood there shaking.

From Wild Fox to Mad Dog and the Road to Freedom

With Gingmai's death, Lek was no longer among the living. She was merely going through the motions. She wanted to know how her beautiful baby died so she took blood samples to have them tested. When she took them to a lab, the lab refused to test her samples. She had to convince a friend to perform the test. He worked in a government lab so he tested the blood in secret. He confirmed the worst: Gingmai died of cyanide poisoning. This explained his bizarre, chaotic behavior.

Cyanide acted to prevent his body from using oxygen, effectively suffocating him to death. As the poison took control, his brain function lessened and the pain got worse. That he could recognize Lek at all was a miracle considering cyanide acts so quickly. Lek planned to use the lab report to go after those responsible. But her friend would only tell her the result. He refused to provide a written report. He had a family to worry about.

When the local newspapers learned about Gingmai's death, reporters began to call Lek. Would she go public? Was she going to speak out about Gingmai's death? Did this mark the end of her exile?

Still suffering greatly from the death of her baby, Lek issued a bold, even reckless public statement under the circumstances: Gingmai's killers were cowards. If they really meant to hurt her, they were cowards to go after a helpless baby elephant.

She went to the police and asked for an official investigation. They told her that only human poisonings could be investigated. That was ridiculous. Anytime a neighbor killed a neighbor's chicken or pig, police were there. If nothing else, it was destruction of property. But it was an expected response given Lek's standing at the time.

Lek cried for three days following Gingmai's death. She wanted to be left alone. She retreated to the pond where her baby tried to drown the effects of the cyanide. On the third day, she felt something poke her. It was Hope. He touched her face with his trunk and felt her tears. His little intervention startled Lek back to reality. A guilty feeling came over her. She had not prepared milk for Hope and Jabu in those three days. Her volunteers told her that neither orphan was taking milk from them.

Something either snapped or something fell into place. Hope reminded her that she was his and Jabu's caregiver. They were her responsibility. If the shadow forces could kill Gingmai, they could also target her other two baby orphans. It was at this, the lowest point in her life that Lek decided to act. She did a remarkable thing; she walked away. Not away from her problems, but from Sakorn's farm. She told her volunteers to pack everything. No one was going to hurt her two remaining orphans. They would go somewhere where they would be safe.

Her first thought was to load Jabu and Hope into a truck. With Hope it was no problem. But Jabu was deathly afraid to step inside the back of a truck. Lek tried time and again, but each time she brought Jabu close to the ramp leading into the truck, Jabu ran away. She even put Jabu's favorite fruits inside the truck, thinking he would forget his fear long enough to approach the food. Hope ate them faster than they could get Jabu near them. Finally, Lek decided to walk.

This was another defining moment in Lek's life. Either she would run away and continue the life of a fearful fugitive, or she would follow Noom's path to dignity, and Phong Sri's mantra to stand up for her beliefs. When Gingmai died, Lek's dreams of being an elephant conservationist could die with him, or she could live to fight for what she believed in. Babies Hope and Jabu represented the lives of elephants she must defend.

In her childhood, the taunts and teases of her classmates making fun of her poor hill tribe background turned her into a little bundle of energy willing to fight back. Now, all grown up in 2003, Lek faced not taunts but real threats to her very being. The shadow forces did not know who or what they were dealing with.

The Elephant Lady of Thailand

Lek and the two babies set out for Baan Lao early one morning. Before they began, Lek spent a few minutes at the grave of Gingmai, talking with her baby one more time. Then she prepared the food and drink that she and two baby elephants would need for an all-day journey. Both orphans were pretty much weaned off milk, but she still had to take along milk bottles filled with water.

After telling the volunteers to pack, she walked away from the pig farm. She headed toward Baan Lao. She was not alone. Two elephants, Hope and Jabu, joined the mad dog. It was a thirty-mile journey along the main roads. But Lek did not follow the roads. She walked with her babies along an old trail used by peddlers.

Hope was the first to show how happy he was. He walked quickly, with an excitement children have when they go on their first long trip. He could not know that he was leaving the only home he ever knew for the last time.

It was hot so the pace was unusually slow. They took breaks near a stream or waterfall just long enough to take a swim and cool down. It was hard to get Hope away from the water once he got in. But they pressed on toward Baan Lao.

The orphans discovered so many new things along the way, things they could never even imagine on the pig farm. And they were free, with just the open road and many side roads to explore. Nothing held them in any more. Even finding new bugs and new kinds of lizards excited the youngsters. But when one species of new bug made a loud sound, Hope ran screaming to hide behind Lek.

When they passed near villages, kids came out to greet them. Hope, more than Jabu, always seemed willing to stop and play with them. Lek stopped in the late afternoon to let Hope take the afternoon nap he was accustomed to. Hope tried to use Lek's lap as his pillow, but he was too big, so Lek sat close to him with her arms around him. While Hope slept for nearly an hour, Jabu played and ate. On they walked, mile after mile, eventually trekking up a mountain until they reached Baan Lao.

When they arrived, Hope collapsed into an all-night sleep, worn out from such an exciting day. Lek built a shelter for her two surviving orphans. No one was going to hurt them. This was her home, her territory, and strange men in uniforms could not enter without several pairs of eyes watching their every move.

From Wild Fox to Mad Dog and the Road to Freedom.
[Dirt road leading to Baan Lao]

Forces Come Out of the Shadows

The attacks against Lek did not end with the death of Gingmai. Thailand's largest newspaper, the *Bangkok Post*, published an article in mid-December 2002,[5] claiming that the phaajaan video released to PETA was a faked ceremony created by Lek. When a major newspaper marshals the forces of journalism against one person, the effect can be devastating.

The article, "The Memory of Elephants," began innocently enough. It described in detail the phaajaan video released to the world, and at least initially, seemed to support the cause of PETA. It was written as a pro-animal rights, elephant-friendly article. But as it continued, the attacks on Lek began. By the end, Lek was demonized as a liar and cheat, someone who tried to fake the phaajaan for personal gain.

The story behind the *Bangkok Post* article began with two people, husband and wife, associated with an animal rescue organization, at least in name. When Lek presented her side of the phaajaan video story in television interviews, the wife called her, demanding that Lek retract her account. She ordered Lek to give an interview to her husband; someone she claimed was well

---

[5] *Bangkok Post*, 15 December 2002, "The Memory of Elephants."

connected to powerful government forces. He was also connected to the newspaper. When Lek refused to give in to the pressure, the article appeared.

The article contrasted two, starkly different ways of training elephants, of making them tame and docile to humans. The first was illustrated in the phaajaan video. Using this "tough and cruel approach," elephants reach the safe phase in days. To use the other "normal, merrier way of training," apparently referring to positive reinforcement, would take "up to five years." Returning to the phaajaan video, the article described in detail hooks being driven into the body of a baby elephant, blows being rained down upon the animal, and even close-ups of blood coming from the baby's ears.

Then, appearing in the article were suggestions about the video's true meaning. "An official who saw the entire video said a woman's voice is heard on the soundtrack." According to the article the woman says, "Beat them harder, more severely." Following this were reports from unidentified Karen villagers who questioned the video. The video according to these sources seemed phony because it did not portray the phaajaan practiced according to tradition.

The article justified the phaajaan ritual, declaring that it had nothing to do with "performing tricks, playing football, or circus acts." In fact, it claimed that "there is no international cruelty involved." The "tradition" was only intended to teach baby elephants, to protect them from harm, and to make them safe when they live with humans. "Further," the article stated, "baby elephants are naturally curious, and, if they are not trained properly they can die from snakebites or accidents."

The newspaper article included a local villager's perspective that the ceremony of phaajaan was not cruel, but necessary so elephants could be loved. "I lived with elephants since I was born. My father gave all the elephants to me, and now I am giving them to my children."

After this defense of phaajaan, the article revealed its true purpose. One section began with the title, Make Believe Film? Lek was named, identified as the Thai woman who took two foreigners to the village to film the phaajaan ceremony. The video was a hoax. Several conservation groups were mentioned, lending more credibility to the truth of the attack against Lek. A ranking member of an organization called Friends of Asian Elephants (FAE) questioned the motive behind the video and whether "a person or any particular group of people is trying to achieve anything constructive."

When government men tried to persuade the shaman in charge of the ceremony to testify against Lek, they failed. The shaman's version was the same as Lek's. It was the shaman's son who yielded to the pressure or money and lied about Lek. In the *Post* article it was the elephant owner's son who was quoted. He said that he was instructed by Lek "to beat the baby elephants more and heavily."

In one lengthy news article, the power of the press through Thailand's largest newspaper was coming down on Lek with full force. The journalist who spun this tale seemed to be skilled in weaving seemingly credible eyewitness accounts with well-known animal rights group testimonials. In a way it was a journalistic work of art; more importantly, it was nothing but lies.

"FAE felt the film was not a true traditional elephant weaning ceremony," the article said.

The article invoked the authority of two powerful national institutions, the police and parliament: "Meanwhile, two committees under the House of Parliament concluded their investigation of the incident and turned the case to the National Police Office, which issued a statement that 'there was no real brutal act against elephants; it was all a total faked-up filming.'"

A police report was referenced in which Lek was accused of directing the phaajaan participants, asking two men to "sit on the back of the elephant and beat the elephant hard with the hook." This section of the *Post* article was entitled, "A Bucket of Blood." It claimed that Lek faked the blood seen in the video: "... Mrs. Saengduan produced a bucket of liquid that appeared to be blood. She poured the liquid onto the head and legs of the elephants."

The village source for this lie explained that he followed instructions because "she hired me." The article then quoted this source "and the others involved in the filming" as if they all could be quoted together, saying that "they did not know exactly what the objective was, but 'got the impression from Saengduan that the film will earn money to support the welfare of elephants.'" There was more: "The police investigation has been augmented by parliamentary committee reports. The Ministry of Foreign Affairs announced that police surveys on elephant training...found no act of cruelty against any elephants." Reference to "parliamentary committees" suggested that the senator who tricked Lek had worked behind the scenes to help accuse her. The ambiguous "police surveys" were more than likely nonexistent.

The Chiang Mai press was not any less accusatory. A story ran December 2002, that raised the same claims against Lek as the *Bangkok Post* article.[6] Referring to the phaajaan video released by PETA, the articles stated that "many organizations involved in elephant care could not agree as to whether this was a factual account, with some even going so far as to claim that it had been set up solely for TV sensationalism." The article quoted none other than Lek's sister, Wassana, as an expert: "She said the [phaajaan] ritual is done for a variety of reasons, including maturing the elephant so that it would stand on its own feet rather than following its mother, or merely that it was time to train the baby for its working life, or even that the baby would not breed again until the previous baby had left home."

This is what the elephant lady of Thailand had to endure: attacks from all sides including her own family. None of the reasons why phaajaan was needed made sense. Even if they did, they did not justify the torture inflicted on the animals. The Chiang Mai article made phaajaan seem like just another phase in the maturity of the elephant and quoted Wassana's park manager: "This kind of ritual is similar to sending our children to school for the first time. Many children cry, and try to run after their parents. Elephants are the same."

The network of articles questioning Lek and the phaajaan video filled the pages of the press in the weeks following PETA's call for a boycott in October 2002. The Forestry Industry Organization denied the villagers in the video were

---

[6] *Chiangmai Mail*, 15 December 2002, "TV Documentary Sparks Elephant Torture Debate in the North" by Metinee Chaikuna.

Thai, but distinguished them as "Karen."[7] Mahouts joined with so-called animal conservationists to demand an apology for the fake video: "An elephant welfare advocate, elephant camp operators, and Karen mahouts have accused the United States-based animal rights group [PETA] that exposed the abuse of elephants here of trying to destroy tourism."[8]

Other articles followed.[9] This was not a minor attack, but a concerted effort to deny the abuse and destroy the source of the video, namely, Lek Chailert, the one person in Thailand who stood up for the objects of the abuse. Lek resolved to fight. With the ruthless killing of Gingmai, Lek would not let the evildoers win.

More threats followed. In January 2003 a man she considered her friend invited her to speak at an international conference being held to promote animal conservation. It was the perfect forum to set the record straight about the phaajaan ritual, about the brutal slaying of her baby, and many other things serious animal lovers needed to know. But the person inviting her was just another false friend trying to set her up.

He told Lek how the nation's image was greatly damaged by the PETA episode. If someone with Lek's stature—even if it was tarnished—would speak to the conference with a simple message, that damage could be repaired. The simple message was that PETA was lying about the phaajaan. He told Lek about people who were considered enemies of the government. They were never heard from again. He mentioned the name of a Thai military man, a general, who wanted to see her. Lek recognized the name. He was someone known for his record of *disappearing*

---

[7] *Bangkok Post*, "Link to Torture Video Denied," 19 October 2002.

[8] *Bangkok Post*, "Mahout, Welfare Group Demand Apology for Video," 29 October 2002

[9] *Bangkok Post*, "Authorities Deny Claim of Elephant Torture in Training," with Tourism Authority of Thailand and Forest Industry Organization dismissing the torture claims as "pushed by self-interested activists desperate for funds," 14 December 2002. Also, *Bangkok Post*, "Thai Ministry Counters PETA Claims," 15 December 2002. Similar articles appeared throughout January, 2003. Mahouts organized a protest march on the capital, including seventy elephants, when legislation surfaced that would have banned elephants from the city streets of Bangkok. Those who opposed the efforts of people like Lek were taking full advantage of the campaign against her. See *Bangkok Post*, "Training Not Abuse," 26 January 2003, and "Mahouts, 70 Elephants Begin March to Bangkok," 27 January 2003.

enemies. When you met with him, you were never heard from again!

After what Lek had already been through, her answer came easily. She told her "friend" that she would not speak at the conference. She would only speak the truth. That PETA had lied was not the truth. After she replied, the threats against her did not stop.

On February 6, 2003 a government crackdown on drugs was announced.[10] This was an anti-drug campaign like no other. Prime Minister Thaksin, a native of Chiang Mai, announced that he would eradicate illegal drug trafficking beginning with a three-month, country-wide program.[11] Police were launching their operation using a newly created list of suspected drug dealers. The list contained almost 40,000 names.[12] Lek believed her name was on the list. The next day, February 7th, Lek was transporting a load of bananas for the elephants in a green truck. She was taking them to Elephant Haven, the mountaintop sanctuary she had been running for years. Her driver was negotiating the mountain road in the middle of the jungle when two motorcycles converged on the truck. One of them pulled up close to the truck, took out a gun, and began banging on the truck to pull over.

Lek was petrified. The two men were not wearing police uniforms. All she could think was that they were assassins. She told her driver to speed up. He did as he was told, even though this was a one-lane road meant for traffic in both directions. As he floored the accelerator, he came to an abrupt stop when an oncoming vehicle threatened a head-on collision. When he did,

---

[10] *Chiangmai Mail*, "The Three-Month Drug War Has Commenced" by Supatatt Dangkrueng, February 2003.

[11] *Human Rights Watch*, "The War on Drugs, HIV/AIDS, and Violation of Human Rights in Thailand," July 2004. According to this report, over two thousand people were killed during the first three months of this campaign: "The result of the initial three-month phase of this campaign was some 2,275 extrajudicial killings, which the government blamed largely on gangs involved in the drug trade; arbitrary inclusion of drug suspects on poorly prepared government "blacklists" or "watchlists;" intimidation of human rights defenders;violence, arbitrary arrest, and other breaches of due process by Thai police; and coerced or mandatory drug treatment." Lek's fear of being caught up as a pawn in the government crackdown was well-founded.

[12] *Chiangmai Mail*, "Interior Minister Receives List of Almost 40,000 Drug Dealers," February 2003.

the two men began shouting obscenities at them, demanding to know why they didn't stop as ordered. They claimed they were policemen. They went up to the driver's door and yanked him out of his seat, threatening to beat him.

Lek had come armed, not with a gun, but with a mini camcorder. After hearing the threatening shouts of the two men, she turned on her camera. The men inspected the cargo. One of them accused Lek of trying to hide something in the banana bunches. The other man asked how she could afford such a nice truck. As her camera recorded the stop, Lek believed that she and her driver were going to be shot. Evidence would be planted among the banana bunches. The government could claim another victory in the war on drugs. At very least, she would record as much of the event as possible. A video tape sent her into exile. This one might capture her murder.

A truck loaded with people approached and stopped, unable to get around Lek's truck. Lek recognized one of them as the leader of a nearby village. He asked the men what they were doing. As he did, he recognized one of the policemen. The two were friends. As the two men talked, Lek saw this as her chance to get away. She told her driver to get back in the truck. He started to argue and she cut him off. "Drive now and drive fast," she told him. They left the jungle road and entered a major highway.

Ten miles later they were stopped again, this time by a uniformed policeman. He gave Lek's driver a ticket for not wearing his seatbelt. It wasn't true. Lek guessed that the two men on motorcycles radioed ahead to have the green truck stopped and cited. When Lek went to the police station to pay the ticket, she saw one of the motorcyclists. Lek questioned him about the stop. He said the stop was legitimate. They were looking for a green truck believed to be transporting drugs.

In November 2003, she was still being targeted. It was then, during the anniversary month of her mother's passing in 1998, that she experienced one of the most frightening threats. It was nighttime and she was in a truck driven by her younger brother, Preecha. Also in the truck were Preecha's wife and young daughter. They were on the steep and winding road to Baan Lao, the same road Lek used to walk to get to school as a child. It was also the same road where the logging truck slid off when she was trapped inside the cab, and chains nearly choked her to death.

As Preecha drove up the road, a spotlight suddenly illuminated the truck. Two men waited for them up the road. One flashed the light on them, while the other pointed a gun at the truck. The gun was an assault rifle. Lek broke down. She screamed as loud as she could. "Why? Why do you threaten my family? Take me! Kill me! Leave them alone!" Her little niece began to scream.

"They have a child with them," said one of the attackers. The men backed off. Preecha drove on.

There were other incidents. Some of the mahouts who worked for Lek were beaten. Vehicles driven by Lek and her employees were stopped and searched. Police even confiscated one vehicle. But something happened in 2003 that would mark the beginning of the end of the campaign against Lek.

The Lady Pet Savior and the Coffee Bean Man

During the tumultuous weeks following the release of the phaajaan video, Lek had little time to dream. Yet, her passion for elephants never wavered. She still wanted to create an elephant-friendly, elephant-safe refuge just as she had begun for Mr. N., and as she planned in 1995 when Elephant Nature Park was first built. The mafia elephant camps destroyed her first attempt when they nearly killed Mr. N. Her own family took control of Lek's Elephant Nature Park, dramatically altering her vision. All she had to show for the backbreaking work she put into the park was the name.

Lek had one more asset, something that seemed out of place considering how much hatred roiled up inside Thailand over the PETA tape. She had her reputation. It was an international reputation for being Thailand's premier elephant lady. No matter how ugly the struggle became inside her own country, her name was still very much respected abroad. Over the years she formed strong bonds with foreign animal rights activists. No one visiting her and seeing her work with elephants could have anything but the highest regard for Lek Chailert. She reached out for volunteers from other countries. She had elephant documentaries made about her work. Her friends included members of the National Geographic Society and PETA. Her media friends came from the Thai television networks, the British Broadcasting Corporation, and CNN. Her television connections extended to programs such as Discovery Communications *Animal Planet*, a program that for years used an elephant in its logo. She may have been the falsely accused enemy of elephant camp owners and other forces in the Thai government, but her standing in the broader community was unshakable.

A year before Lek went underground to escape the threats; she received an international honor for her work with elephants. Ford Motor Company began a program in 1998 to recognize those who made positive contributions to preserving the planet. In 2000, Ford joined the National Geographic Society in conducting a public awareness campaign to sensitize the world's public to critical conservation challenges facing Earth. The campaign was named Earthpulse. In 2001, a Ford Foundation/National Geographic Hero of the Planet award was given to Lek Chailert.

Through such international recognition, Lek enjoyed the friendship and admiration of fellow animal advocates who believed in her work. In December 2002, when the world seemed to be collapsing around her, something happened that defied explanation. After running for her life, after watching her beautiful baby, Gingmai, die in her arms, Lek met two very special people who would change her life, but this time for the good. Jane was the first one.

When Hurricane Katrina devastated New Orleans in 2005, the human toll was enormous. But with it, a large number of pets were left stranded. Katrina hit New Orleans with the full force of a Category 5 hurricane on August 29, 2005. Over fifty levees were breached and over eighty percent of the city was under water. In all, nearly 1600 people died in Louisiana alone. Between 250,000 to 600,000 pets died or were stranded. Tens of thousands were left suffering alone, on the streets, in abandoned houses, and virtually anywhere the flood waters forced them. Animal rescue teams were not allowed into the city until early September, aggravating an already horrible situation. Key animal rescue organizations responded, including the American Society

The Elephant Lady of Thailand

for the Prevention of Cruelty to Animals and the United States Humane Society. State chapters of each national society were also on the scene.

One woman led the animal rescue crusade. Jane Garrison helped create the nonprofit organization, Animal Rescue New Orleans. She was one of the first on-scene commanders to direct rescue efforts that eventually led to thousands of Katrina pet victims being saved. Spending seven weeks in New Orleans, Jane rescued over thirteen hundred animals with her own two hands.

That was in 2005. In December 2002, Jane Garrison visited Lek. During this visit she knew what desperate straits Lek was in. With Jane's connections, another animal lover entered Lek's circle of special people. Bert was a coffee magnate of sorts. He did not grow coffee beans, but was a major coffee bean importer. He was president and owner of the Serengeti Trading Company. He was also an animal lover of the highest order. A parallel organization, the Serengeti Foundation, was established in 1997 as a tax-exempt nonprofit organization dedicated to land and animal conservation. The foundation website states that no member of the organization is paid a salary or even uses foundation money for travel expenses. It sums up its mission in one simple statement: "We're all about saving the land and protecting its animals."

Through Jane Garrison, Bert heard that Lek needed funding for her new Elephant Nature Park. She had the elephants, which she had been keeping at Elephant Haven. She had mahouts who wanted to work for her. And she still pursued the dream of opening a park where the public would pay to learn about elephants, not ride them or in any way exploit them.

In March 2003, Bert traveled to Thailand to see the elephant lady. When Lek went to the airport to pick up Bert, she had her own idea of what he would look like. Obviously, he was an older man, perhaps quite elderly. That is what she expected, an older, well-dressed gentleman. He stepped off the plane and how wrong she was. He was quite young. Instead of a coat and tie he wore casual clothes, blue jeans, and fit no businessman stereotype at all. He had no gray hair or even graying hair, because Bert had a shaved head!

She took him to stay at Elephant Haven where he experienced the rough conditions that humans must endure so elephants understand this is their home. After an overnight stay in the elephant retreat, Lek took Bert on a tour of the land that she wanted to buy to start Elephant Nature Park, or more accurately, Elephant Nature Park II. He said very little. He was the American version of Master Suwan, the teacher who taught Lek how to be strong.

Bert began his interview with Lek by asking two questions: How much land did Lek need to create a decent elephant habitat? How much money would the land cost? Bert's third and final question might have been the most important question of all. He asked her how much she wanted it. And then he was gone.

Lek could not believe what happened. Gingmai was still fresh in her mind. Death threats were still being made. So her disbelief was not unexpected. Besides, she heard similar promises of help over the years. Visitors always seemed so impressed with her program to help the elephants. They told her how much they cared too. They promised to help. And then they returned to their country of origin and nothing happened. Lek thought this might happen again with Bert. She refused to get her hopes up.

There was one difference with Bert. He left with very specific information. He knew precisely what tract of land she needed. She took him there. It was over forty acres with a small river running through it. He knew that she needed six million baht, or approximately $146,000 U.S. dollars. He told Lek something very specific as well. He told her to check the bank account set aside for the purchase of this land in three days. He called her and asked her what was in the account. Lek hadn't checked. When she did, there it was. Six million baht had been electronically transferred into the account. Elephant Nature Park was born again.

The year 2003 was not the ideal year to construct a new elephant park. The first outbreak of avian flu struck Thailand in January 2003. Thousands of chickens had to be destroyed, devastating the country's poultry export market.[13] SARS or

---

[13] *World Health Organization*, Report of 5 December 2005.

Severe Acute Respiratory Syndrome also threatened the country. The combined effect devastated the Thai tourist industry.[14] If this was not enough, the world was reacting to the invasion of Iraq in March 2003. Traveling abroad was less appealing.[15]

Lek pressed ahead. She had conceived and helped build two other elephant parks. To supplement her crippled travel agency, Lek took jobs as guest speaker and university teacher. With the extra money she earned, she purchased food and medicine for her elephants. Foreign volunteers were also hard to come by during this time. At times, she was down to a single volunteer per week to handle any visitors to her new Elephant Nature Park. While the outbuildings went up as planned, only one hut was constructed to house the volunteers.

The national tourist shortage was not the only threat to the survival of the park. Local officials and police continued to treat Lek and her staff as an outlaw elephant camp. Unlike the other camps, this one did not "donate" any money to their cause. One of her employees had his new motorcycle "confiscated" by police. Lek called the police station and complained. The policeman who actually took the bike told her afterwards that he did not appreciate being reported to his superior. He made it clear that he would be keeping an eye out for illegal activity at the park. Lek got the message, but did not budge. Despite frequent visits by police, sometimes arriving in force, and phony inspections, Lek did not yield to the pressure to pay off the corrupt officials.

Elephant Nature Park, as it looks today, overcame constant harassment and survived the drought of tourists in 2003. Lek tried everything she could to make it work. She made jewelry that she sold in the night market of Chiang Mai. Her loyal staff worked for months for virtually no pay. Lek entered the world of real estate transactions and found ways to make profitable deals that let her pour the profits back into her dream. Slowly, her park became profitable. Writers from *National Geographic* and

---

[14] *Diethelm Travel's Thailand Tourism Review,* "Thailand Tourism, 2004-2008." This article indicates a precipitous drop in tourist arrivals in the April and May of 2003 due to the threat of SARS.

[15] *Pataya Mail,* Vol. 11, No. 19, 9 May – 15 May 2003, "Thai Tourists Expected to Salvage National Income Lost After Gulf War and SARS," by Patcharapol Pamrak.

Readers Digest helped the park attract more tourists with articles about the elephant lady.

"Stand like a rock!" – Lek Takes On Powerful Forces

When the largest Bangkok newspaper printed a false story that she fabricated the phaajaan video, Lek sued the newspaper. It took several months for her day in court to arrive. When it did, many Karen villagers went to Bangkok to support her and show the court that Lek never lied and never staged anything. When she saw all of their flip-flops neatly lined up outside the courtroom, she broke down and cried with appreciation.

The attorney for the newspaper tried to intimidate these simple hill tribe people. They never had been in court before. They were poor villagers who came to the big city to testify on behalf of one of their own. In this trial, they were paraded before the world. A veteran lawyer was trying to make them look bad.

The villagers were frightened but that changed nothing. They told the court the truth. They testified that the phaajaan was a tradition and ceremony over one hundred years old. They said that Lek Chailert never put them up to anything. It was a way of life passed down from one generation to the next.

Lek sued the paper because it printed stories that she paid the villagers to stage the phaajaan. She also sued an elephant camp owner who made a public statement that in days gone by someone who did that would be burned or have their throat slashed. Lek wanted the world to know that, as a result of these lies, she lost her baby, Gingmai, her family and friends were harassed and threatened, and she was forced to hide to avoid being killed.

The lawsuit against the newspaper and camp owner took over two years to complete. When she finally got her chance to testify, her opponents' lawyers tried their best to attack her character. They tried to associate her with known criminal elements. They asked her if she knew a particular name, a name shared by the criminal. The lawyer demanded a "yes" or "no" answer. She refused. She fired back, "Who is this person? What does he do?" She would not be led into an elephant blind, trapped in her own words. When she tried to explain her answer by asking the questioner to explain the person she was asking about, the judge began to shout at Lek. But Lek stuck to her guns. She had come too far and waited too long for her chance to prove the newspaper and the camp owner were lying about her. In one exchange, Lek could feel the spit from the opposing lawyer's mouth strike her face as he cross-examined her.

"In 1991, Miss Chailert, you met a Mr. Yai, didn't you?" Lek asked him to explain who this Mr. Yai was. It was a very common name. The lawyer yelled at her, "Don't ask me questions! Just answer yes or no!" The judge scolded her as well.

Lek refused to answer unless they explained who they were talking about. Her opponents were trying to link her to a man caught up in the illegal elephant trade as well as in drug dealing. Lek corrected them, saying she knew of the man, through newspapers and other media, but never met him.

The judge tried to intimidate her, asking if she was familiar with the woman from Hong Kong who fabricated a rape allegation. The woman went to prison. His message was easy to understand: Lek, if I believe you are lying, you will go to prison. Lek told him she was the one looking for justice. She was the one who brought this lawsuit because others lied. He was attacking the wrong party.

Great pressure was placed on Lek to drop her lawsuit, but there was too much at stake. The newspaper asked to settle the case by issuing her a private apology. She refused the offer. She told the paper's attorney she didn't expect a complimentary article about how wonderful she was. All she wanted was for the paper to publish a truthful story about what Lek did for elephants. The paper told her to write the article and agreed to publish it. Again, she rejected the proposal. She insisted that a senior journalist be assigned to write a truthful article or there would be no settlement.

To this, the newspaper agreed. The writer came to her, apologizing at once. Lek showed him the fifteen elephants she cared for. Then, she asked him how she could ever get money to pay villagers to stage a phaajaan. He had no answer. She told him to write the truth about the practice. PETA released a tape she shot at one village. But, she explained to him, she had witnessed the practice at many other places.

It would not be the last article the paper would ever publish that told the truth about Lek and the phaajaan. But it was the first. It did appear. She was vindicated. She did not sue for money. She sued to get her dignity back. She won. But it was not completely satisfying. Nothing could ever bring back Gingmai.

She won another case against a newspaper in her own region of Chiang Mai. The court made the paper publish more articles that told the truth. In one of these, the writer labeled Lek the angel of elephants! The newspaper apologized for failing to find all available facts before publishing inaccurate stories about Lek.

She did not win all of her lawsuits. The elephant camp owner she sued hired one of the best-known lawyers in the region. He was able to have his part of the lawsuit dismissed. But win or lose, Lek stood up for her name and reputation.

2003: From Hunted to Admired – The Genesis Awards

Lek Chailert traveled down the most dangerous of paths in 2002. But as dark and terrible as the journey became, she clung to her simple hill tribe notions of honesty, hard work, and kindness to those with less. She followed the lessons of Grandfather Noom. She inherited the courage of Phong Sri. When Jane Garrison helped her find a benefactor in Bert, Lek forged on with her dream. Just as Bert and his foundation gave her dream new life, the international community, including a powerful American connection, rewarded Lek for what she had accomplished over the years.

The Genesis Awards were created by a pioneer in animal conservation. The late Gretchen Wyler created the program as a project for The Fund for Animals. As a member of The Fund's board for twenty years, she helped expose animal cruelty practices occurring around the world. Because of her own star status, being an accomplished actress, singer, and dancer, she used the Hollywood spotlight to further The Fund's animal advocacy.

Each year the Genesis Awards precede the Oscars. The ceremony is a glamorous, star-studded event held in Beverly Hills, California. The awards recognize the work of writers, directors, producers, journalists, and all those involved in the news and entertainment media whose work contributes to better public awareness of animal issues. When Gretchen Wyler began the Genesis Awards in 1986, less than two hundred people attended. Seventeen years later the ceremony had grown tremendously.

On February 25, 2003, the list of award winners was announced by the Hollywood office of the Humane Society of the United States. Gretchen Wyler was then still a force, serving as the vice president of the Hollywood office. Over twenty winning productions were announced after surviving a seventeen-member selection committee. The winners included American Broadcasting Company's *World News Tonight* and a feature about whaling, *Animal Planet*'s "Animal Cops," the *U.S. News and World Report* feature "Cruel and Usual," and a local television report, "Inside the Cage." Each winner was recognized for increasing public awareness about animal rights and animal abuse. There was one special winner. This was the official Genesis Awards Guest of Honor. It was Sangduen "Lek" Chailert, honored for her work with elephants.

It was a great honor for Lek. It meant so much after the turbulent year where her life was at risk, and her beloved Gingmai was poisoned. The Genesis Awards would take place on March 15, 2003. The problem was how to pay for the trip. Lek only had three hundred dollars saved. That is all she and Adam had saved from operating Gem Travel. Actually, it was less than that. Before she left, she paid her staff and bought milk for her elephants.

Even though she and Adam were no longer married, they still looked out for each other. Adam would accompany Lek to Hollywood. Their travel and hotel accommodations would be paid by the sponsors. But how could she afford the daily living expenses of Hollywood? She vowed to eat very little on the trip. Adam helped her prepare an acceptance speech. She was not a natural public speaker, and speaking in English in front of a large audience was extremely demanding.

Once in the States, Lek's self-doubt took over. The past year was the most tumultuous of her life. She lost her mother and her precious Gingmai. For several months she lost her own identity, hiding from those who considered her a national disgrace. She literally had to start over, building a new elephant park from scratch. She was living day-to-day, scraping and scrambling just to get by. Life was so incredibly strange. How could she possibly deserve such an award? She was on the red carpet of absolute splendor among the glittering lights of Hollywood. All she could do to overcome her feelings of inadequacy was to think of the one person in her life who would want her to stand tall. She had to show her friends and her enemies that this little hill tribe girl was strong. Phong Sri expected nothing less.

Lek went to the awards presentation with two people: Adam and Phong Sri. Beneath the glaring lights of the International Ballroom of the Beverly Hilton Hotel, she was escorted to the podium by real live Hollywood stars. Actor William Baldwin stood nearby. Gretchen Wyler presided over an audience of nine hundred for a program that would reach millions via television.

Jennifer Hile, one of Lek's close friends, won a Genesis Award for her award-winning documentary, "Vanishing Giants," a program that focused on the dwindling elephant population in Asia. Jennifer worked closely with Lek to reveal the awful truth about elephant abuse. She was there with Lek as she worked to save Gingmai. She filmed street elephants in Bangkok. It seemed so fitting that Jennifer would win for the film she produced for the National Geographic Channel and Lek was the guest of honor for the entire ceremony.

Lek was led to the podium by a beautiful Hollywood movie star. Lek was dressed in a simple but beautiful native dress, representing her hill tribe background. She was introduced as the best hope for saving the vanishing giants of Thailand. Behind her was a special set featuring a huge elephant surrounding and almost devouring the stage. When her name was announced, the room seemed to explode with applause. This didn't help her nerves. A bad case of stage fright took over. Adam's speech had been loaded into a teleprompter. Either it did not work, or Lek was so shocked that she did not see it.

The audience seemed to clap forever. As they did, Lek's eyes filled with tears. Somehow, despite the need to focus on her words, and in the middle of a thunderous welcome to the microphone, Lek thought only of her mother. How she wanted her mother to be there to see how well she had stood like a rock.

When Lek's mind finally returned to the awards podium, she still could not stop the crowd from clapping. She searched for the right words to tell them to stop, but nothing came out. All she could do was take her hands and move them up and down, like a wave. Eventually they got the message and all eyes and ears turned to the tiny moonlight girl from Baan Lao.

She told her audience how fortunate she felt to be able to speak on behalf of the elephants. For years she thought of herself as the voice of abused elephants who could not speak for themselves. Now she could do just that. She told them she hoped they understood her English. She made them laugh with her. But she could not talk long. She was overcome with emotion and lost the power to speak. So, in closing, she simply thanked the audience. They responded with more grateful cheers and applause.

Lek won other awards, but 2003 was the year of her rebirth. In that year, she rebuilt Elephant Nature Park and operated it according to her original beliefs. With the help of the Genesis Award, the forces that tried to stop her lost out to the international recognition of being Thailand's premier elephant conservationist.

In 2005, *Time Magazine* named her an Asian Heroine of the Year. The magazine wrote about her courage in the face of so many challenges: "Chailert and her staff have been threatened and harassed by less humane animal park operators, and she believes, local officials in league with them. Masked men have menaced her on the road, and local papers labeled her a traitor for publicizing the elephants' plight. Nonetheless, she says, 'I can't turn my back on them. I can look in their eyes and see fear. Somebody has to stand up for them.'"

The local Chiang Mai press included a glowing article on the work that led to this award.[16] The award was presented on November 23, 2005 in Taipei, Taiwan.

In 2006, she was awarded an honorary Ph.D. in veterinary science, presented by the Crown Prince of Thailand.[17] It was

---

[16] *Chiangmai Mail*, "Sangduen Named Asian Heroine For Her Work in Elephant Conservation," 15 October 2005.

[17] *Chiangmai Mail*, "Park Founder Receives Honorary Ph.D. from Crown Prince," April, 2006

given to Lek "in recognition of her longstanding work for the environment, and of course, the animals under her care." Over 5,000 people attended the Chiang Mai University event.

In 2006, she was given an Earth Day Award. In 2008, she received the Outstanding Woman of Thailand Award.

Since building Elephant Nature Park in 2003, Lek Chailert has remained steadfast to her mission of saving abused and injured elephants in her native Thailand as well as anywhere in the world she is asked to go. The operation of the park is explained in photographs and video found on the internet.

As of the date of this book's publication, Lek Chailert continues to organize Jumbo Express missions throughout Asia. As any westerner whoever accompanied her knows, Lek's work always involves an element of danger. The danger comes not from her beloved elephants, but from the many treks through the jungle to get to those elephants. In the spring 2009, she traveled to Myanmar to work with logging elephants. During that trip, she was bitten on the face by a spider, one known for its deadly venom. Both of her eyes were swollen shut. When she tried to board a plane to return, the airline refused to allow it, thinking she might die onboard. She had to have a trusted friend travel from Thailand, meet her at the airport, and then wrap her head so that her swollen face could not be detected.

Every March 13, designated as National Elephant Day, her staff and volunteers seek to educate the people about the need to protect the endangered elephant population. This is nothing new for Lek. During a 2002 Elephant Day campaign, she offered her vision of what must be done: "If elephants are going to survive in Thailand then the law of the land must change…"[18] Without legal protection, the abuses practiced against elephants will continue. Elephants will lose their natural life cycle. Lek continues to work to save elephants and return them to their natural environment. Her work represents the power of one woman against great odds.

---

[18] *Good Morning Chiangmai*, "Spotlight On A Symbol," March 2002.

The Elephant Lady of Thailand

Genesis Awards: Lek was led to the podium by one of the beautiful Hollywood female film stars. She was dressed in a simpe but beautiful native dress, representing her hilltribe background.

Genesis Awards: She told her audience how fortunate she felt to be able to speak on behalf of the elephants. For years she had thought of herself as the voice of abused elephants who could not speak for themselves. Now she could do just that.

Epilogue

A little hill tribe girl, perhaps seven years old, ran up the mountain, away from the creek, back to her village of Baan Lao. She was frightened beyond belief. She ran full speed until she reached her mother's arms. No matter how hard she tried, she could not get the word out. All she could do was stutter the first sound of the hill tribe word for the huge animal, not *seuua*, the Thai word, but something closer to the sound of a cat, *meow*, which is how a little girl speaking kham muang dialect describes a huge cat.

After several tense moments, Phong Sri understood what her tiny daughter was trying to say: *tiger*. A special alarm made of hollowed-out bamboo was sounded. Villagers knew instantly what this meant. Children playing outside were pulled into their little village homes. All doors were shut. A group of men with guns was dispatched to patrol the area.

A week later, Lek again saw the tiger, but this time in a much different way than when she saw him at the creek. This time his legs were tied to a long pole and four men carried the pole back into the village. The giant beast's jaws were wide open in death. Lek felt a rush of guilt, guilt over causing the death of this magnificent jungle creature. She would learn, from her shaman grandfather, a very special rule of that jungle: don't harm animals and they will not harm you. It was a guilt and a rule that others in the world did not feel or follow.

Author's Note:
A Chance Meeting at Elephant Nature Park

In June 2007, I went to Thailand with my family. My wife was born there. I felt our two grandsons, at ages nine and thirteen, were old enough to learn about their grandmother's Thai family and see firsthand the tiny village where she grew up. In planning this trip, I decided the boys should see as much of the country as possible. Our vacation would take them to the capital of Bangkok, into central Thailand, in and around Korat, and finally to Chiang Mai in the mountainous north.

In trying to show them everything important about Thailand, the idea of letting them see or ride elephants seemed like the right thing to do. I entered a few words into a search engine: elephant tours; elephant parks; elephant trekking; and so forth. Whatever I entered, Elephant Nature Park came up as one of the links to try. As I began comparing treks and tours, national elephant parks and private parks, I kept coming back to Lek's Elephant Nature Park website. There were companies that offered elephant rides. Others described elephant shows and the tricks tourists would enjoy, tricks like elephants dancing to music, or painting pictures with their trunks. Only Elephant Nature Park stood for saving abused elephants and educating visitors about them.

I made reservations at Elephant Nature Park through the internet. We spent our first two days in Bangkok, adjusting to a completely opposite time zone. Next, we visited Korat and my wife's village of Dan Khun Tod, an hour's drive from Korat. After that it was back to Bangkok where we boarded a "sprinter" train to Chiang Mai. The train did everything but sprint. This was a twelve-hour train ride through the heart of Thailand, from the lowlands around Bangkok, to the mountain jungles near Chiang Mai. It seemed to stop a hundred times on the way to Chiang Mai, but that's exactly what I wanted so my family could experience more.

In Chiang Mai, an Elephant Nature Park van picked us up at our hotel. After collecting other tourists at their hotels, the van stopped at a market to buy fruit. This was not for the tourists, but for the elephants. All of the tourists helped load a truck full of bananas, watermelons, and fresh corn. An hour later we arrived at the park.

It was there that we saw the foreign volunteers, dedicated workers who helped run the place. Some taught the visitors about elephants. Others worked in the fields. What happened throughout that one day became a lesson to me and my family that no amount of formal schooling could ever teach. We were there not to ride or be amused. We were there to observe the elephants brought to recover from injury and abuse. We would all take part in feeding them. We also would follow them down to the river and take part in their elephant baths.

As the day unfolded, I saw a small Thai woman in a straw hat, walking in the high brush, sometimes next to an elephant, sometimes alone. She seemed to be tracking the movements of the visitors. She seemed shy and most comfortable at a distance. It was Lek. After a few hours doing what all of the other visitors did, I saw Lek sitting in the main hut, talking to tourists. I sat near her and struck up a conversation.

I asked Lek if anyone had ever written about her life. She told me there were several articles and even promises by some to write a book. No one actually followed through. I told her I was very interested. I spent all of fifteen minutes with her.

We returned to the States and I could not stop thinking about this accidental meeting at this rather randomly selected tourist stop. The concept of an elephant park that did not offer rides or tricks, but only education, was such a refreshing one. I sent an e-mail to Lek through her park's website, asking if she would be interested in letting me tell her story. At the time, I knew only as much as her website told me about this hill tribe woman.

Someone on Lek's staff intercepted my message, and not thinking it was important, did not pass it on to Lek. Some weeks later, I received an e-mail from Lek, apologizing for not answering my message. Somehow she found it. It was all a big mistake. From that moment on, Lek began sending me material to write this book.

In December 2009, I again traveled to Thailand to conduct interviews with Lek and to visit various places I needed to see in order to describe them. I spent another day at the park. She took me to Baan Lao where I saw the house she had built for Phong Sri. I saw the building where the Hmong opium eaters bought their drugs. I visited the treacherous mountain road where a logging truck went barreling down a mountainside with Lek wrapped in chains, nearly killing her. Lek took me to see where Master Suwan taught her and the other little pigs. I saw the banyan trees that held the ashes of Noom and Phong Sri. I went to Noom's special place of meditation, on top of a mountain, where one could spy the Karen village where Noom saved the son of the village leader. After this visit, my research was complete. And it all began by a chance visit, or did it? Steeped in jungle lore and surrounded by the spirit of Noom, chance may have had nothing to do with it.

To say that this experience has changed me is a great understatement. I no longer see any useful purpose to circuses and zoos. I question why any country allows wild animals to be sold as pets. I realize that for any object made of elephant ivory, there may be a story of death or excruciating pain for the animal that lost the tusks to a poacher.

The author and Lek with villagers on top of Noom's special mountain of meditation.

Special Footnote: Lek Goes to Congress.

In October, 2010, Lek Chailert was among the invited honorees in Washington, D.C. for their work in bringing awareness to the ongoing damage to the Earth's environment. This special recognition was hosted by Speaker of the House, Nancy Pelosi and members of the Congressional Caucus for Women's Issues.

"Lek Chailert of Thailand earned the enmity of tourism companies when she publicized the suffering and abusive treatment given to elephants, which are often forced to perform for tourists in the country." Bureau of International Information Programs, U.S. Department of State.

The Elephant Lady of Thailand

A week later Lek again saw the tiger, but this time in a much different way than when she saw him at the creek. This time his legs were tied to a long pole and four men carried the pole back into the village.

Photos from Today's Elephant Nature Park
[www.elephantnaturepark.org]

The Elephant Lady of Thailand

Printed in Great Britain
by Amazon